CARIBBEAN WOMEN
AT THE CROSSROADS

CARIBBEAN WOMEN AT THE CROSSROADS

THE PARADOX OF MOTHERHOOD AMONG WOMEN OF BARBADOS, ST LUCIA AND DOMINICA

Patricia Mohammed
and
Althea Perkins

Centre for Gender & Development Studies
The University of the West Indies, Mona Campus
UNFPA/International Planned Parenthood Federation
Western Hemisphere Region, Inc
Research Project Report, 1997

Canoe Press
University of the West Indies
Barbados • Jamaica • Trinidad and Tobago

Canoe Press University of the West Indies
1A Aqueduct Flats   Mona
Kingston 7   Jamaica

03 02 01 00 99   5   4   3   2   1

CATALOGUING IN PUBLICATION DATA
Mohammed, Patricia.
Caribbean women at the crossroads : the paradox of motherhood
among women of Barbados, St Lucia and Dominica/
Patricia Mohammed and Althea Perkins
p.cm.
Includes bibliographical references and index.

ISBN: 976-8125-44-6

1. Women – Decision-making – Barbados. 2. Women – Decision-
making – St Lucia. 3. Women – Dominica.
I. Perkins, Althea. II. Title.

HQ1525.43.M64   1999   305.04'0972981 dc-20

This publication has been funded by the United Nations Fund for
Population Activities (UNFPA) through the International Planned
Parenthood Federation, Western Hemisphere Region, New York

Set in StoneInformal 10.5/14 x 30
Cover and book design by Robert Harris
Printed in Canada

Contents

List of Tables / *vi*

Abstract / *vii*

Introduction / *viii*

CHAPTER 1   Research Design and Methodology / *1*

CHAPTER 2   Profiles – Barbados, St Lucia and Dominica / *15*

CHAPTER 3   Socioeconomic Overview / *33*

CHAPTER 4   Analysis of Data From Questionnaire / *44*

CHAPTER 5   Selected Life Histories of Women
From Barbados, St Lucia and Dominica / *82*

CHAPTER 6   Official and Unofficial Views / *96*

CHAPTER 7   The Dynamics of Decision Making in the
Lives of Caribbean Women of Barbados,
St Lucia and Dominica / *110*

Bibliography / *127*

Appendixes

I   Recommendations / *129*

II   Questionnaire / *131*

III   List of Interviewers and Official Sources
in the Three Islands / *136*

IV   Map of the Caribbean showing Barbados,
St Lucia and Dominica / *138*

Index / *139*

List of Tables

Table 1:   Age of Respondents in the Sample / 44

Table 2:   Marital Status of Parents of Respondents / 46

Table 3:   Educational Level of Respondents in the Sample / 48

Table 4:   Migration History of Respondents / 54

Table 5:   Age at Which Respondents Became Sexually Active / 58

Table 6:   Marital Status of Respondents in Sample / 60

Table 7:   Number of Children of Respondents in Sample / 61

Table 8:   Age at Which Respondents Had First Child / 62

Table 9:   Methods of Contraceptives Used by Respondents / 63

Table 10:   Person who Made Decision Regarding Type of Contraception Used / 63

Table 11:   The Most Important Decisions Women Have Made in their Lives / 68

Table 12:   Major Obstacles to Achieving Goals / 74

Table 13:   The Kind of Life Women Would Like to Have / 77

Abstract

The following study is an exploratory one, examining the dynamics of decision making in the lives of Caribbean women of Barbados, St Lucia and Dominica. The study uses as a base the responses from a questionnaire administered to 375 women in the three societies, together with a selected number of oral histories drawn from this sample. These data are analysed alongside a series of interviews with officials in family planning and development agencies in each of the societies and other documented material relevant to the subject. The aim of the study is to understand what factors affect the decisions women make in the major events of their lives. The key areas which we set out to examine included their education, job/career choices, selection of partners, marriage, timing and number of children, abortion, immigration and involvement in extracurricular activities. The issue of decision making was also conceptually linked to the process and the determinants of women's aspirations. Thus the study was concerned with the social, economic and cultural factors which influence or inhibit the choices available to women within these societies. Women find themselves faced with dilemmas of choice between a career and other aspirations which include partnership and children. Caribbean women are now at the crossroads of choice.

Introduction

The main objective of this study, commissioned by the International Planned Parenthood Federation (IPPF), Western Hemisphere Region, is to explore the dynamics of decision making related to the major events in a woman's life and the major influences affecting the process and the determinants of her aspirations.

The study aims:

a) to provide new insights into the key motivating factors in Caribbean women's lives which would assist family planners in designing programmes appropriate to their needs, aspirations and specific circumstances, and

b) to contribute research data which is specific to women in the countries of Barbados, St Lucia and Dominica.

Some of the factors predetermined for investigation in women's lives were: selection of partners, marriage, timing and number of children, abortion, job/career choices, education, immigration, and extracurricular activities.

The phrase "dynamics of decision making related to major events in a woman's life" leaves the researcher open to a large number of research questions and issues which can be focused around two central concerns:

1) What are the key dynamics in decision making in women's lives? Do women have autonomy in controlling their decisions or are these circumscribed from birth by parents, class, spouse, and the social and cultural expectations of women in the particular society?

2) What are the focal points or major events in women's lives around which important decisions are taken? What do women themselves determine as the major events in their lives? How do these decisions tally with the aspirations they set for themselves in life? Do they have a calculated set of goals which informs the choices they make?

The process of decision making may differ for women by age, class, level of education, parents' occupation and so on. For instance for a younger woman of the contemporary generation, education and career may be of primary importance, for a woman of nearly completed fertility of a previous generation, wifehood and or motherhood may have been of primary importance in her youth, with her own priorities shifting with additional life experiences.

While the ambit of the study is that of the dynamics of decision making in major events of women's lives, the research issue which links decision making to aspirations is itself a very broad based one, requiring both an empirical analysis of the choices which women make, and a logical appraisal of the process by which decisions are made. To carry out this multilevel task, the research begins with certain assumptions and ideas and simultaneously incorporates different methods of gathering and assessing data.

The first major assumption is the premise that Caribbean women of all territories are more similar than different, sharing common cultural ideas on femininity together with a collective notion of the possible choices available to women in the region. Previous research and understanding of the English-speaking Caribbean have revealed many basic similarities resulting from a common historical legacy. While drawing on the similarities found across the generic Caribbean region, the study seeks to determine if there are differences by society as a result of size and level of "development". It attempts to investigate if there are distinct differences due to geography, size and historical precedents and how these affect the formation of class structure, access to careers and other opportunities, and thus of women's perception of themselves in the specific societies researched.

The constructions of femininity in the region were variously stereotyped – the strong and independent black woman, in control of her economic, social and sexual life, comfortable with her familial role, and politically motivated in the anticolonial and nationalist movements. This is contrasted to the European bourgeois ideal of the middle class dependent housewife and the elite ladies of leisure who were generally coloured or white. The stereotypes accorded to men in these societies placed them either as marginal to the home and family or as breadwinners with patriarchal control over women and children and state processes. These fixed stereotypes misrepresent the life experiences and choices available to women in the Caribbean. This study seeks to deconstruct the stereotypes and to see the real individuals behind the constructed image.

Research Design and Methodology

A Retrospective Literature Review[1]

A study by Edith Clarke, *My Mother Who Fathered Me*, first published in 1957, pointed to some key factors which influenced the pattern of family organization in the Caribbean. Clarke's work developed out of a critique of a previous study by R. T. Smith on Guyana [1956]. In his study of the Negro[2] family in Guyana, Smith coined several generalizations which came to typify our understanding of the lower class West Indian family. These can be summarized as follows:

a) "Common-law" unions and legal marriage were sociologically identical and it was neither necessary nor appropriate to distinguish between them

b) Caribbean males were marginal to their families, in that children derived nothing of importance from their fathers who were ineffective, even when resident within the families

c) Most or all Negro "lower class" households are "matrifocal" and dominated by women in their combined roles of mother and wife. Female domination increases as children grow up and as daughters reproduce the same patterns of their mothers

d) This notion of matrifocality continued to the subsequent extended families or household in which grandmothers, mothers, daughters and their children continued to live and share resources and lend emotional support to each new generation.

---

[1]The focus of this review is primarily that of the African/European descended population. The situations of Trinidad and Guyana differ as a result of wider ethnic and cultural variations within these societies where a larger Asian community reveals different family types and a more patrifocal than matrifocal culture.

[2]The terms such as Negro, lower class and concubinage are retained in this review as they were used in the original studies. These terms have undergone shifts in terminology now and will be appropriately addressed as this study continues.

The exclusion of non-residential mating and offspring as valid family forms, and the conflation of household structure or union type – particularly legal or residential union with "family" – signalled a clear message to Caribbean peoples themselves. It intimated that the ideal typology of the European "nuclear" family somehow represented the normative. Thus it confirmed the notions that family typologies, union types, community values, and regional variations which derived from the particular internal histories and specific socioeconomic conditions of each society were aberrant forms. Edith Clarke's contribution represents a departure from this reading of Caribbean family systems.[3] Clarke's study was based specifically on the African lower class family in Jamaica. She demonstrated how alternative types of mating systems influenced the constitution and stability of household groups. Variations in organization and character of local communities are associated with significant differences in the patterns of family structure which are observed. While Clarke's findings, as the title of her book suggests, maintained a dominance of matrifocal families among women of lower socioeconomic strata, her analysis sets the stage for identifying *first*, differential stages within any one woman's life, and *second*, how differences in local systems of mating inform and underlie differences in domestic and familial organization of varying Caribbean communities. Edith Clarke's insistence that the economic preconditions and correlates of marriage contrast to that of concubinage, may not have been far from the reality of these matters, even as we investigate women's lives in the Caribbean today. In addition, Clarke argues that "in fact there is no apparent real association of marriage and concubinage with the economic status or class structure", an insight which bears greater relevance to the determination of women's status position in contemporary Caribbean society.

Informed by the colonial ideology of the period and still heavily influenced by the anthropological discourse of the time, the preoccupation with class structure and status, with legal unions and nuclear families as the ideal type, and with a Christian morality informing the tone of the writers, the dilemmas and choices of the subjects of these discussions – individual women and men – and the power relations between individuals in families and households, did not constitute a major part of these discussions. Not until the 1980s do we see studies that begin to sift through the meanings of the stereotypes which described Caribbean family forms and the status of women in the region [Mohammed 1988].

The process of recovering women's lived realities began with the data accessed by the Women in the Caribbean Project (WICP). The WICP was a comprehensive two and a half year project (1979–1982) developed as part

---

[3]Family studies provide the primary source of data on women in the Caribbean for the decades of the 1960s and the 1970s.

of a programme of policy oriented research within the Institute of Social and Economic Research at the University of the West Indies. The programme sought to assist decision makers within the region, and was conceived essentially as a device to expand the empirical knowledge and understanding of the reality of the lives of women in the Caribbean, "and to contribute to the process of identifying policies and programmes which could address and alleviate some of the problems which women face". The focus was on women, the methods and content were interdisciplinary, ranging from historical research on education, to field surveys on women's familial, domestic and work roles. The latter were carried out in the countries of Barbados, Antigua and St Vincent. From this source of data, published in several forms, we can begin to examine some of the research issues which this study also investigates.

Joycelin Massiah noted in an introduction of the project document that:

like women researchers in many regions of the world, WICP researchers were faced with the situation that knowledge of women's experiences in their region has been filtered through studies and methodological tools designed, conducted and interpreted by males. Personal experience and knowledge of their communities persuaded the group of researchers involved in this project that a more accurate picture could be obtained by addressing issues other than the structure and function of family groupings. The major objective of the project was therefore to identify the subjective meanings of the social realities which women face, the way these realities are manifested and the consequences at the individual, community and societal level.[4]

An attempt was made in the WICP study to place women's issues in specific historical and developmental contexts, particularly important in a region where slavery, colonialism and political independence were crucial in shaping the conditions of both women and men. The country studies in Barbados, Antigua and St Vincent pointed out immediately that one of the greatest single problems facing women in all three territories was that of unemployment, which particularly affected women of a lower education and social status. The limited possibilities for occupational choice and consequently greater dependency on either kin or spouse restricted the extent to which autonomous decisions could be made. Added to this was the pervasive ideology surrounding women's roles, the subsuming of individual needs to that of parents, spouse and children. While attitudes to spouse or mate varied, childbearing and the care of children emerged as a central theme in women's lives.

The age of the population sampled in the WICP was between 20 and 64. Childbearing was found to be one of the few areas of Caribbean women's lives which is not "surrounded by ambivalences" [Senior 1991: 66]. Olive Senior, in *Working Miracles: Women's Lives in the English-Speaking Caribbean*, points to what she calls the universal impulse to mothering as evidenced from the data of the WICP. Senior observes: "Although women today have greater options

---

[4]Joycelin Massiah, "Women in the Caribbean Project: an Overview", *Social and Economic Studies* 35, no. 2 (1986), 1.

through education than their mothers and grandmothers ever dreamed of, the view persists that the real vocation for women is motherhood." Dorian Powell who examined the initial data of the WICP on childbearing also concluded that "It is through childbearing that women realize their self image: there is the conviction that women ought to have children" [Senior 1991: 66]. Senior's evaluation of the WICP data confirms that despite the "sexual revolution" and the loosening of parental influence, especially in urban areas, in many cases old behaviours and ideas still apply. "In her constant exposure to conflict between what she is told and what she perceives around her, the young girl is also being subjected to strong pressures in a society which presents her with few alternatives to childbearing" [Senior 1991: 76]. Part of this pressure comes from other and older women, part from boys or older men, all of whom exploit the young girl's ignorance and superstition.

Apart from the mythical and biblical injunctions that assert the importance of childbearing and the griefs of childlessness, for women themselves mothering a child is deemed a marker of femininity. More rational reasons, nonetheless, account for the centrality of childbearing for women. Children focus and order women's lives, absorb their emotional capacity especially in the context of an indeterminate relationship with the male. Children are also seen as a pragmatic resource for old age. While the WICP data confirmed a high correlation between education, employment and fertility, it is clear that for all women, the factor of childbearing must be demarcated as a primary one around which other variables can be assessed.

This insight is confirmed by another finding of the WICP. Christine Barrow points out that

Within Caribbean society, women and men in conjugal unions retain considerable autonomy especially in economic matters. While affection may be part of many unions, the more binding type of love is concentrated within the mother child relationship. Women are quick to claim emphatically of their partners "He ain't no family to me: I bore no pain for he" [Barrow 1986: 138].

She points out that most women change partners at least once during their life cycle, and even married women express uncertainty about the future of their unions. The importance of marriage or a recognized stable union may be secondary therefore to the issue of childbearing among Caribbean women.

A third issue considered by the WICP which has relevance to the present study is that of "Power and Decision Making in the Household". While this study examines decision making in a more generalized framework of women's lives, clearly the crux of the issue is the extent to which women actually have power to make decisions in their own households and within the wider societal framework. The findings of the WICP here are instructive. Regardless of the still dominant patriarchal ideology of the culture, there emerges a positive relationship between women's resource earning capacity and power in the household. Nevertheless the perception of this varies by type of union. Thus "married women perceived decision making structures to be largely egalitarian while women in common-law unions perceive them as largely woman-dominated". The study, however, found variation between one territory and the next in this respect, with Antiguan women protesting a much more male dominated presence in decision making than the other territories of Barbados and St Vincent. The extent to which power is real or perceived is not explored by the WICP study and it signals another area of investigation for this study – to pursue this point as a key to understanding if Caribbean women in fact strategize around a myth of male dominance but in effect have great control over their lives, as long as they have the resources to do so.

A fourth and related point is the status position of women as workers in Caribbean society. Despite internal changes in various Caribbean societies, domestic tasks are primarily allocated to women. There is also a high level of female activity in agriculture and in other lucrative areas of industry largely organized by women themselves in the informal sectors of production and marketing. This high level of female activity does not imply that men are correspondingly involved in a low level of economic activity. What it implied was a high visibility of women as workers, reinforcing the points made by Smith and Clarke that the image of the Caribbean woman was one of a worker with independent means of providing for her offspring.

The findings on Caribbean women as workers both inside and out of the home have led to different theoretical understandings of gender relations in the region. Applying the public/private dichotomy of gender spheres, Patricia Anderson depicts four features which typify women's gender roles in the Caribbean. Women support their own families with household and extra-household work, and achieve influence through their domestic and maternal roles. She suggests that status, however, is achieved through their affiliation to men. In other words they defer to men's decisions in the public realm, and exercise power only within the households [Anderson 1986: 291–324]. The work of Christine Barrow, Constance Sutton and Susan Makiesky-Barrow suggests that the conventional assignment of public roles to men and domestic roles to women is a stereotype that does not fit the Caribbean reality. These researchers demonstrate that Barbadian women are neither confined to domestic units and linked to the outside world through men, nor are they submerged within kin groups. They posit instead that there is an overlap between community and domestic spheres, rendering the public/private dichotomy limited in the case of the Caribbean.

Perhaps what is being articulated in these two interpretations are the different experiences of some women's lives in the Caribbean, where public/private dichotomy has less relevance. To others, such as women of the middle and upper classes, the dichotomy may be of some significance, but only if we continue to assume that these women do not also perform valuable tasks necessary to the well being of the family and therefore to society.[5] Perhaps the fundamental question which needs to be asked is why has a superior role been attached to the public and a subordinate one to the private? Studies such as the present one clearly need to begin unravelling the real meaning of this dichotomy for women who have always been workers outside of the home and simultaneously within the home. For women who have chosen or been obliged to work primarily within the domestic sphere, does this relegation confer on them a lower status? Is motherhood and being a housewife a mark of female underachievement in society? These questions will persist as part of the definition of femininity and the valorization of woman in society and cannot be resolved in this study. What is important is that as researchers we are aware of these ideas as they influence women's perception of themselves and thus the choices they make. Furthermore, this awareness must also inform how we as researchers perceive our research subjects, therefore what we make of our data, and consequently how our analyses continue to shape women's images of themselves and the definition of their gender identities in the region.

A fifth issue, following directly from the last, pertains to the changing self-image of woman in the Caribbean, which may itself be a major factor in the dynamics of decision making today. Joycelin Massiah writes of Caribbean woman:

Historical material indicates that following emancipation, women of all races became involved in various sectors of the economy. Better education and involvement in an ever widening range of economic activity presented women with the opportunity to affect alternative images of womanhood and to achieve a measure of independence [Massiah 1986: 226].

While some women may have benefited, there is still variation by social class and level of education. Nonetheless, the perception of a range of possibilities which have become available is no doubt one of the features that characterize contemporary society: the changing image of woman and the ideological and programmatic shifts in women's condition which have taken place universally over the last three and one half decades have begun to influence the choices which women make in their lives.

Another recent collection of essays entitled *Women and Change in the Caribbean* [1991], edited by Janet Momsen, develops some of the themes which are interrogated in the present IPPF survey. In her introduction, Momsen makes the following observation:

Within the Caribbean regional diversity of ethnicity, class, language and religion there is an ideological unity of patriarchy, of female subordination and dependence. Yet there is also a

---

[5]This point is developed by Mark Figueroa in his work on conceptualizing "social capital". He argues that women's contribution to capital development cannot be quantified primarily in terms of surplus value, but must also be viewed in terms of the non-quantifiable resources such as discipline and emotional security which contribute to production. See for instance his paper "Does the Market Undermine its Social (Resource) Base?", Department of Economics Seminar Series, University of the West Indies, Mona, Kingston, Jamaica, 1995.

vibrant living tradition of female economic autonomy, of female-headed households and of a family structure in which men are often marginal. So Caribbean gender relations are a double paradox: of patriarchy within a system of matrifocal and matrilocal families; and of domestic ideology co-existing with the economic independence of women.[6]

Momsen makes the insightful observation that despite the importance of much of the previous work on the situation of women in the Caribbean in extending our understanding of gender relations and gender roles in these societies, "it has provided a somewhat unidimensional view of the women of a multifaceted complex region" [Momsen 1993: 3]. Thus the ideology of gender in the Caribbean region until recently has continued to be one of female independence and male marginality, which has worked against the interests of women themselves. The notions of independence and strength have created further disregard for the special needs of women within households. They influence development policy which interprets this to mean that women do not need to be treated separately as a group, for access to goods and services, in areas of their lives which are differently affected to men. While the studies cited above have clearly attempted to investigate the continuous changes in the region as a result of shifts in migration processes, changed economic circumstances, the impact of increased access to education, more choices in occupational roles, and greater power in decision making at many levels, it is vital that contemporary studies pay attention to the salient factors which have bearing on the lives of women as distinct from men.

Elsa Leo-Rhynie points to some of the changes which have taken place in the Jamaican context which mirror developments taking place in other Caribbean societies. She notes the improvement in attitude towards use of birth control methods and the importance of both career and family to women [Rawlins 1987]. In addition, she summarizes the following factors which have been responsible for changing attitudes among women – these include the appreciable decline in family size and the extended family networks, the exploitation of educational and economic opportunities available to women, the increase in property ownership of women, that women are conscious that even where men are present they assume headship of the family, and that female headship is generally related to ownership and higher income than their partners. Leo-Rhynie also notes the importance of migration for women in the decade of the 1980s, a marked reversal of the previous trends which were male dominant.

In light of the above discussion, several considerations inform the theoretical framework which underpins the research process and data analysed for this study. These are:

---

[6]Janet Momsen, Introduction in *Women and Change in the Caribbean: a Pan-Caribbean Perspective* (Kingston: Ian Randle; Bloomington: Indiana University Press; London: James Curry, 1993), p.1.

1) The traditional approach to the study of the woman within the confines of family and the understanding of the family itself as a "natural" and universal institution has concentrated the analysis of women's lives on externalities rather than on the internal dynamics of choice, or the bargains which women make with their partners, extended networks and children.

2) Few studies have sought to determine individual women's needs, to locate a micro-approach to decision making among women. Decision making has been viewed either as beyond the control of the individual woman, and located in the structural and ideological factors which predetermine individual choices in a society, or has been generalized around an assumption that as largely "matrifocal" by definition, Caribbean women do indeed have a great deal of control over their decisions.

3) A third factor which clearly bears more relevance to contemporary research is the articulated self-consciousness of gender identity which has been emerging in the region since the 1980s but which clearly has become more pronounced in the 1990s. The ideas of "matrifocality", strength and independence of women were formulated within a framework of antagonistic gender relations, with the notion that somehow women created the material of their lives only in relation to the real or imagined "marginal" Caribbean male. This categorization has undoubtedly served women well in some ways, conferring on Caribbean women a tradition which was antithetical to the received European ideology of the weak and dependent female character. Both interpretations of femininity were, nonetheless, a natural corollary of the way in which women were traditionally viewed in society – as an adjunct to a dominant patriarchal male. Femininity or feminine gender identity could only exist in relation to masculinity, the latter also taken as a given. The present discourse on gender has created a new dimension in our understanding of the correlation between femininity and masculinity. While there is clearly an ongoing and negotiated relationship between men and women within households, in their intimate relations, and in the wider society, the concept of equality articulated in the feminist discourse requires us to examine femininity as also existing as an identity forged by women themselves, in relation to other women, changing with each historical period and varying in different cultures. It can be argued that the shifting perception of femininity and actions of women are some of the factors compelling a redefinition of masculinity.

Perhaps the most important shift in the last two decades of the twentieth century has been the notion of individual achievement which is the entitlement of either sex. The struggle for sexual equality has been a persistent one before the twentieth century, accelerating in the latter half of this century. While this struggle began with a notion of equality and sameness between the sexes, it has been forced to recover the essential differences between male and female. Women undoubtedly still desire, and have always desired, to establish harmonious relations with a male partner or make their own choices in sexual partnership. A greater selfconsciousness of individual gender identity has, however, generated another predicament – that greater freedom carries its own responsibility. While freedom has its disadvantages, it also brings advantages and can benefit women in terms of their own aspirations for life, the ideas they cherish of self-fulfillment and personal growth – above and beyond partnership and childbearing in many cases.

The main issue we are presented with in the cultural context of the Caribbean region is that the typecast of "matrifocality" has been an ambiguous one for women. Apart from being too sweeping a generalization to make for women of all races and classes, it does not take into consideration differences in personalities and predilections of individual women. Matrifocality is perceived as independence and strength when it is convenient for women to be treated as similar and equal to men, for instance when both are field workers. At the same time as far as power and decision making are concerned, though still viewed as "matrifocal", in the public sphere women are treated as different and less capable. A further problem with the generalized assumption of matrifocality for all women is that it confers an additional burden on the articulation of their needs in the Caribbean, both at the level of policy and in the sphere of intimate relations. In other words, in the double paradox which Janet Momsen refers to above (of patriarchy within a construct of matrifocal and matrilocal families), if women are strong then they do not need the help of their male partners; if they are resilient, then when they are left without either emotional or financial support, they will "bounce back"; if they are perceived as largely heads of households, then social policies also treat them accordingly as having power in their decision making within households. Is this the case of Caribbean women in the dynamics of their choice?

The present study attempts to continue demystifying and breaking down these stereotypes of "woman" in the Caribbean. It also challenges the placing of generic "woman" primarily in the family, by focusing on the specificities of women's lives in areas such as career and personal history, the latter including education, migration and extracurricular activities.

Research Design

This study involved a survey of 375 women, 125 drawn from each of the participating territories of Barbados, St Lucia and Dominica. The proposed method of enquiry involving considerations of feminist methodology[7] requires first a statement of some of the parameters of the study.

---

[7]See for instance the concerns of feminist methodology, which focuses on the "standpoint" of woman as discussed in Sandra Harding (ed), *Feminism and Methodology* (Bloomington: Indiana University Press, 1987).

First, with regard to the population to be targeted for interviews, since the study feeds directly into family planning programmes, it is clearly rational to limit the female population to those women of childbearing age, between 15 and 44. The upper age limit is a useful one to investigate as the completed fertility and life experiences of older women may contribute more to the overall question of how decisions are taken by women, than using a sample which deals primarily with those on the threshold of major decision making.

Secondly, the category "woman" has to some extent been used thus far unproblematically. There are differences in perception as to what comprises women's roles between younger and older interviewees. The increased efforts of women's rights movements and intervention policies for women over the last two to three decades have had a major, if undocumented, impact on the attitudes and perceptions of younger women. While this is a pre-tested assumption here, it is necessary in entering this study to appreciate that the way women make decisions is based on the possibilities which the society allows them at any time. Even within the structured ideology and constrained by opportunities available to "the female sex" we must also appreciate that women have persistently defied expected norms and forged new identities which they configure as femininity, and they use this to their advantage and for the benefit of those around them.

The manner in which Caribbean women have historically made their decisions, the choices they have been forced to make, as well as the new forms of coping which they have defined for themselves, have not been fully researched or appreciated. The study therefore begins with the following assumptions, hypotheses and within the established parameters.

Theoretical Parameters

This study focuses primarily on women, using women's voices as its main empirical source. Woman as a category is viewed as central to the study and given agency in determining notions of femininity. The status of woman and the position of woman in society is not viewed as contingent on the male, whether he is father, spouse or partner. This does not mean that femininity is viewed in isolation from masculinity, nor does it mean that the views of men are ignored in the study. The study also relies on interviews or other data collected from and about men, which give further insight and expand the findings. Male interpretations are necessary to examine the dynamics behind the perceived "antagonism" between the two sexes and to understand how women negotiate within the societal frameworks which confine them to certain behaviours and expectations required of the female in the particular society.

The second theoretical parameter is the shift which is slowly taking place in the traditional public/private dichotomy. While it is clear that there is a patriarchal dominance in political power and decision making at the level of the state and public policy, the study attempts to view women's work, whether it is childrearing, cooking, washing or doing accounts for a firm, as all productive work, work which contributes to the welfare of society, if not to surplus production of capital in the neo-classical economic sense.

The third theoretical issue which follows from the above is the definition given in this study to the key phrases *the dynamics of decision making* and *aspirations in the lives of Caribbean women*. Literally applied the phrase "dynamics of decision making" suggests the forces which produce motion, or change motion, and, "aspirations", the strong desire to achieve something, a goal which, in this case, women perceive as their future. In other words, we are investigating what women do with their lives, what choices they make, and why they make the choices they do in the light of the goals they set for themselves and their children.

Methodological Parameters

The age group of women surveyed is that between 15 and 44, and represents lower and middle income women rather than those drawn from the upper income groups in these societies. The women are likely to range between African and mixed/African descent, those of African descent representing the dominant ethnic groups in the societies chosen. The survey and oral historical research carried out for the three territories allow us to provide some evidence of the complexity of choice, and to examine the differences between the life chances available to women in the various territories.

Major Hypotheses

1) Childbearing and childrearing still represent the major events in the lives of most Caribbean women. These may be perceived as "natural" roles around which other choices in life are organized. Decisions pertaining to work, career, family, spouse or partner, extracurricular activities and migration revolve around the centrality of childbearing.

2) The importance of childbearing as a primary definition of femininity in the Caribbean may be simultaneously undergoing change among different groups of women in the society. Women who choose higher education and careers make more deliberate and conscious choices about deferring childbearing or setting a context for childbearing, as for example with a stable partner and within a stable union. This difference may be more marked for a younger group of women than for women over a certain age threshold.

3) Women of different class or income groups have different levels of control over their lives and autonomy in decision making. Lower income women may be allowed greater freedom to flout social norms in order to exercise certain choices than women of higher incomes or education levels. But

women with higher education and more career opportunities have the wherewithal to autonomously make some choices not available to women in low income brackets.

4) Women of all ages and socioeconomic groups are gradually shifting their concepts of femininity to incorporate notions of self-fulfillment and self-actualization of their individual goals. This may or may not include the definition of self in relation to partners; either way this is a deliberate and conscious choice on the part of women themselves.

Research Methodology

The methodology adopted in this study is a three-tiered one.

First, a nine-page questionnaire, containing fifty-nine open ended and closed questions was administered to 125 respondents in Barbados, St Lucia and Dominica. The questionnaire was designed to elicit information on education, career history, migration history, and personal history, including extracurricular activities of each of the persons interviewed. A sample questionnaire is included as Appendix 1 of the study. The questions in each of the areas cited above explore the key areas assumed to be of major importance in women's lives, applying a number of checks and balances within the questionnaire to arrive at some understanding of the dynamics and process of decision making.

The questionnaire was administered by trained interviewers selected from each of the three societies. The selection of the interviewer from each territory ensured familiarity with the region and allowed for the nuances of culture, language and idiom in the individual territory. An attempt was made in the training of interviewers to direct them to a wider selection of persons to be interviewed, across age groups, different socioeconomic status and dispersed over the rural/urban divide. In selecting the sample of 125 respondents from each society, the interviewers randomly chose those who were contacted and agreed to be interviewed. Where interviewers worked, for instance as community workers in St Lucia, they drew some of the sample from districts in which they would normally carry out their duties. The sample can therefore be described as a purposive sample and clearly by no means a representative sample of the populations investigated. The sample constituted 0.04 percent of the population of Barbados, 0.08 percent of the population of St Lucia and 0.17 percent of the population of Dominica.

The sample was also weighted on the side of the population of women who use family planning clinics or who are organized in other activities where women are to be found congregated. The sampling procedure allowed us to attempt a cross-section of the age structure, socioeconomic status, and rural/urban distribution of the population but again makes no claim to an entirely representative distribution of the women in these categories in each society. Both the time and budget allocation for the study limited the range of participants in this project. The sample of women finally chosen was selected on the basis of availability. Then, while the interviews were accumulating to 125 the sample was measured for representation of age, education, career and employment situation. Housework was considered as work even where women said they were housewives and did not work. Union status was also considered as a variable which applies to single, married, visiting or common-law relationships so that both attached and non-attached women were taken up in the final sample of 125 in each society.

Data were collected from three main sources and in two phases. Each source and phase of data collection provided another set of material and ideas to enhance analysis. The initial phase was that of selection and training of field interviewers and the collection of the first source of data derived from the administration of questionnaires. The questionnaire provided the chief source of primary data and was viewed as a valid expression of women's own experiences and desires.

The subsequent phase involved the collection of the second source of data which consisted of taped oral history interviews carried out on a selection of the women to whom questionnaires were administered, as well as from other women who agreed to taped interviews. The collected questionnaires were analysed and collated, and the major findings of these were again pursued in another set of oral histories. A total of twenty-three oral history interviews were carried out, ten in Dominica, seven in St Lucia and six in Barbados. In this second phase of longer in-depth taped sessions, the questions pursued by the interviewers were informed by the findings and preoccupations of the first questionnaire. It also allowed the researchers to understand the pattern of women's lives, which although sought in the questionnaire, did not necessarily follow a chronological flow of their experiences. This was particularly important for the objective of the study – to assess the dynamics of choice and to pursue the hidden meanings which women attribute to daily experiences which they see as natural and individual challenges. The oral history interviews, in addition, tally with the methodology being prescribed by this study for research on women's lives. They facilitated a conversation with the interviewee rather than the impersonality which results from pen and paper.

A third source of data was the collection and analysis of primary and secondary, qualitative and quantitative information. The qualitative and primary data source here was that of taped or untaped interviews with personnel in family planning clinics and associations in the three societies. These interviews provided the opportunity to see how policies and programmes which target women were being translated into practice in each of the societies. Appendix II shows a list of names of the interviewers as well as officials interviewed in the three islands. The secondary data comprise demographic surveys of population, labour force, education, fertility reports and ephemeral material such as newspaper articles, reports on the status of women, and other social surveys carried out in each of the territories. This overview of the socioeconomic data is variable due to the unavailability of comparative information on all issues raised. Nonetheless, the overview establishes a useful framework for analysing collected survey data. The qualitative data source is that of photographs of contemporary society of Barbados, St Lucia and Dominica. This need to incorporate visual material arose from the researchers' field visits to the islands, visits which conveyed the vast differences in the three settings.

Limitations and Strengths of the Methodology

There are limitations in the methodology, despite the checks and balances imposed on the data gathering process. First, the interviewers in each of the territories were clearly different, having different interpretations of various questions and varied styles of interviewing. Second, the focus of the study is primarily from a micro-base, focusing on the testimonies and narratives of individual women and individual professionals in these societies, rather than matching this data with a vast array of quantitative and qualitative sources from a macro-level (as for instance an in-depth analysis of wider socioeconomic trends in migration, cultural specificities or political economy). Thus the analysis is restricted to the observable and articulated viewpoints of the persons interviewed, backed up by accessible pre-collected data.

Perhaps the main strengths of the methodology used in this study are first, the theoretical framework which challenges the public/private dichotomy and the notion of what constitutes work, and second, the significance given to the responses of the women who were either questioned or interviewed. Because of the smallness of the sample, it was possible to treat the data from the questionnaire in both a quantitative and qualitative way. Correlative analysis was carried out manually as it allowed an intimate knowledge of the survey data. To some extent the method of analysis used privileges the qualitative over the quantitative, employing both the positivist method of objectivity of data with strengths of predictability, reliability, and numerical valuation, with that of the anthropological method of observation and ethnography. Incorporating the ethnographic methods allowed us to garner the additional insights gleaned from travelling to a territory, and learning firsthand some of the problems or opportunities which our respondents had. In this way we drew on standpoint feminist methodology of identifying with the women in the territory we were studying. We are also women who have lived and negotiated with the circumstances presented to us in Caribbean society.

Profiles – Barbados, St Lucia and Dominica

Barbados

St Lucia

Dominica

Barbados – 1995

Views of Broad Street, Bridgetown, capital city of Barbados

◄

Typical middle-class suburban housing in Barbados. Transportation provided either by privately owned vehicles – fairly late models of cars – or by an efficient bus system

◄

Barbadian shoppers have a choice of local or imported goods in well stocked supermarkets

► A grandmother in Barbados looks after her daughter's child while she is at work

► The tourist industry in Barbados is a major source of employment for young women, as well as for older women

Dual roles of Barbadian woman: professional jobs and motherhood

Dual roles of Barbadian woman: professional jobs and motherhood

▶
*Mr Charles
Pilgrim:
Executive
Director,
Barbados
Family
Planning
Association*

''Barbados has a well developed infrastructure, a literacy rate of 98.2 percent and compulsory education to age 16 . . . In secondary schools, there is a lack of achievement among males. Girls are more academically inclined, boys have other interests like football. More and more women are deciding not to get married. One professional well-educated woman in Barbados announced that she wanted a child, but had no intention of getting married. This influenced the behaviour of many people.''

St Lucia – 1995

◄
Ministry of Community Development, Castries. The newly emerging face of the main city

◄
A busy street scene in Castries. Informal economic activity co-exists with formal shopping facilities. The presence of vendors everywhere bears witness to an active street life

▶ *Temporary vending facility on Jeremie Street, Castries, St Lucia, paying homage to Derek Walcott's birthplace*

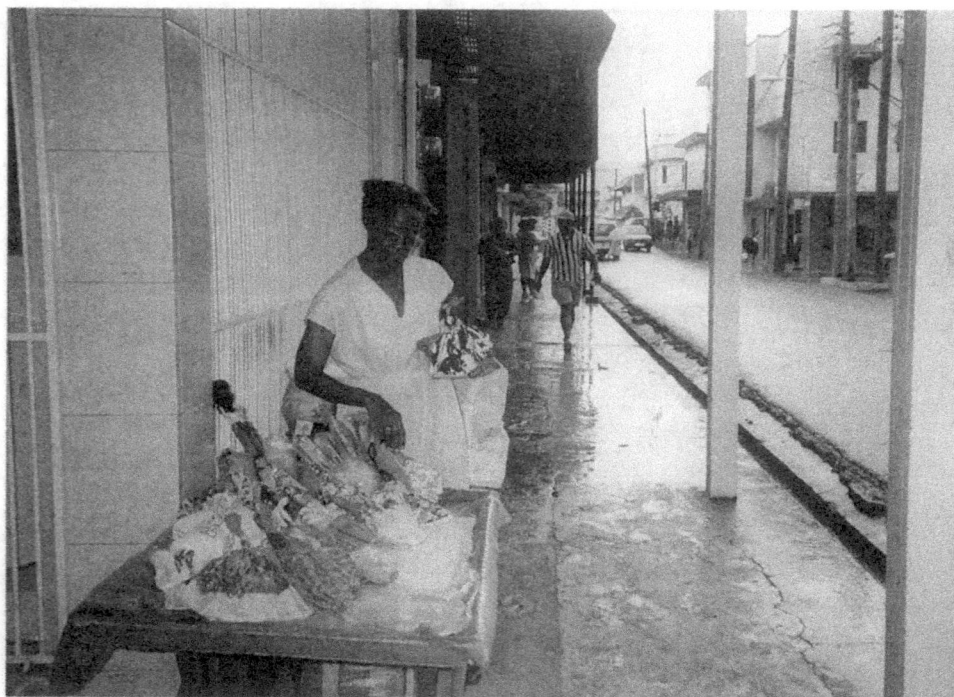

▶ *She makes and sells these St Lucian dolls at EC$15.00 on another street corner in Castries*

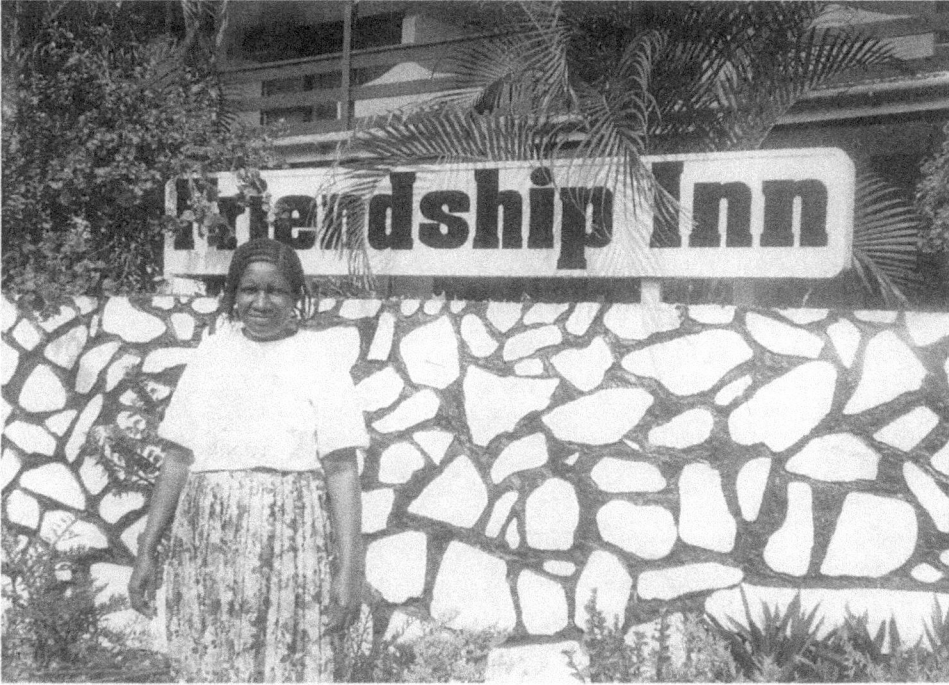

◄ Tourism provides a large number of jobs for St Lucian women. Andrea decided to work for her own wages as housekeeper at this guest house where her family had grown up

◄ Cecilia Prospere, one of our interviewers in St Lucia is a highly trained, very cooperative and committed community development officer. With a very supportive family she manages to mix both career and family more happily than many Caribbean women we spoke with

▶

*Mr Jim Xavier
is a commu-
nity develop-
ment officer
and one of
the field inter-
viewers for
this project in
St Lucia*

"In St Lucia, since more women than men are completing tertiary education and choosing careers, contraception has become one more conscious choice they are making in
their lives, particularly since the 1970s. Women have learnt more control through
education."

▶

*Mr John La
Force: Director,
St Lucia
Planned
Parenthood
Association*

24

Dominica – 1995

◄

Two main streets in Roseau, capital city. Old wooden buildings and slow, unhurried traffic are still to be seen in this picturesque old city

◄

Roseau is set against the backdrop of hills which everywhere dominate the rural and urban landscape

► Mr Willie Fevrier: Director, Dominica Family Planning Association

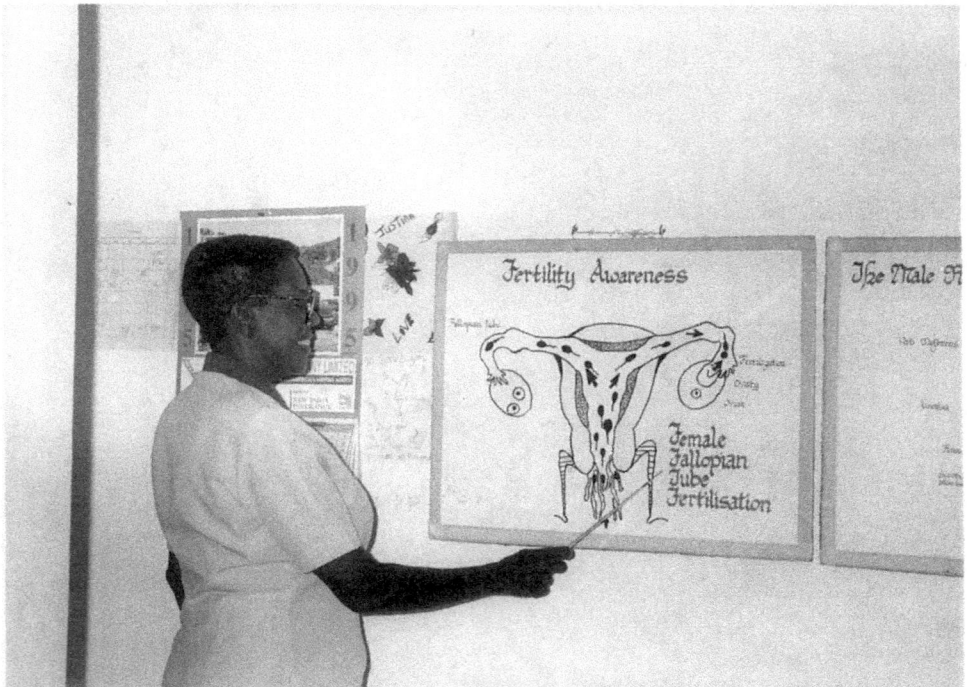

► Women in Dominica do not see men as an "automatic part" of their lives. There are many examples of women who are greater achievers than men in Dominica

An urban market produce seller plies her goods just outside one of the main supermarkets in Roseau – sticks of cinnamon bark, mangoes and citrus

▶ *Dominican women get up and go. Nurse Grell (far right), family planning educator in Dominica, meets with a group of young women at one of the community sessions*

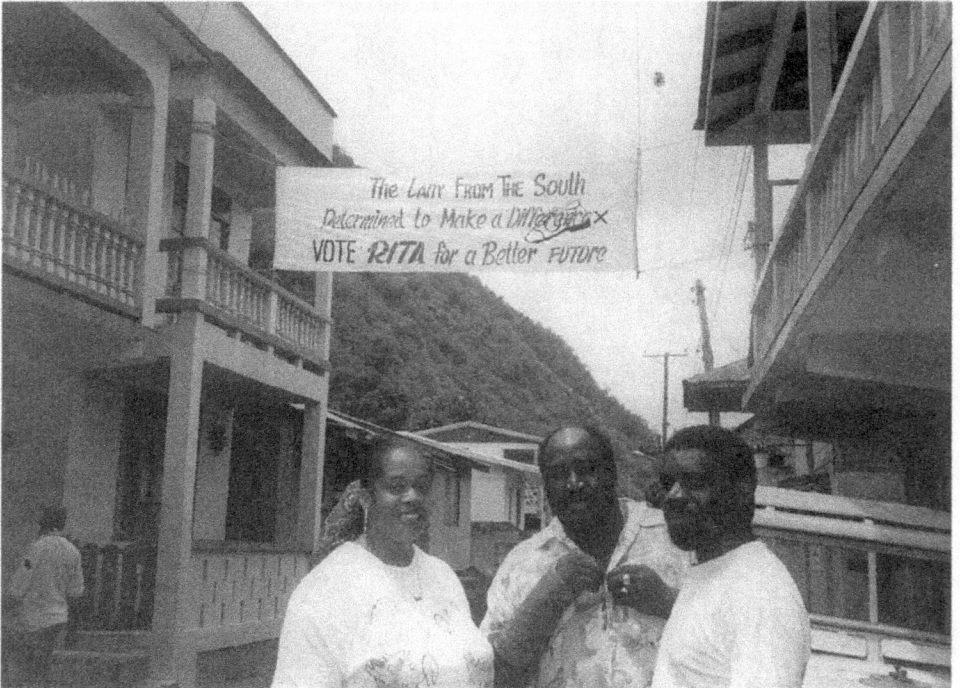

▶ *Rita, a candidate for the upcoming election, campaigns with a banner across the street. Two supportive men are confident of her success*

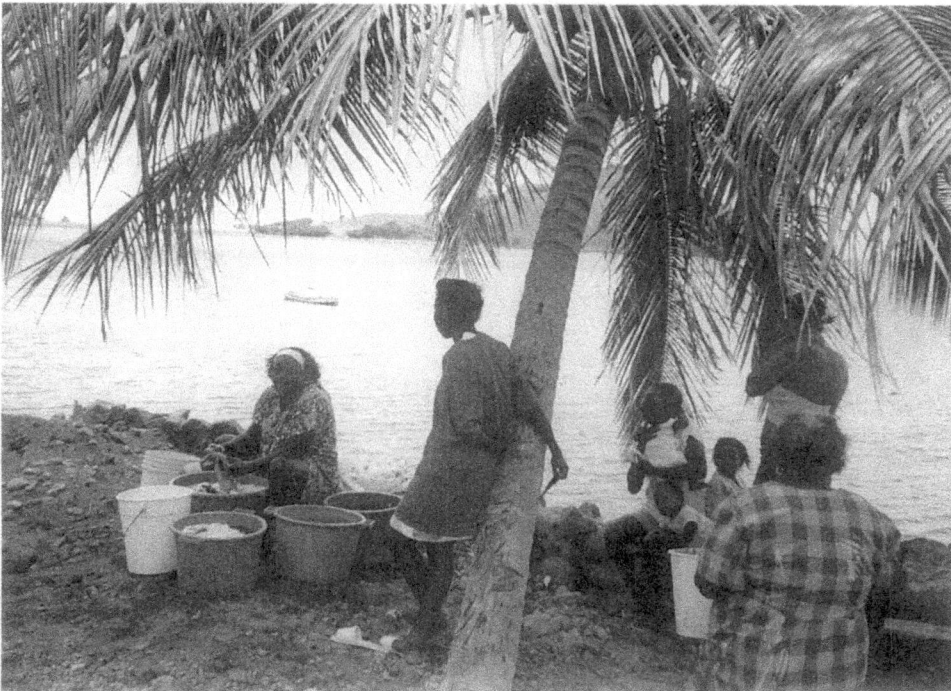

Women's work in the rural districts, combining washing and childcare

▶

Two glimpses of male activities in Dominica. The young man takes a heavy load on his head in Grand Bay. The old men pass the time sitting near the beach front in Grand Bay

▶

Two young girls in Do- minica can still enjoy a day on the beach. Deci- sions and chores can be deferred until later

"Childbearing is important for a woman. Education as aspiration is not always fully satisfying. Many women had children when they were not ready but must have one child. I think they make a conscious decision that they want at least one child and when they want to have it but this does not always work out. More women are deferring childbearing to find job or career because with a job they can earn and purchase what they want, including independence."

Socioeconomic Overview

The opportunities and choices available to women in contemporary Caribbean society are a product of history and the ongoing relationship which these territories have with each other in the region and with global developments.

The wider Caribbean region includes English, Spanish, French and Dutch speaking territories, some of which are islands situated in the Caribbean Sea, others are located on the land masses of South and Central America. There is a wide range of spoken languages which include not only the above four major language groups, a legacy of the colonial past, but also indigenous tongues or mixed languages such as Papiamento and Patois. The ethnic populations include African, perhaps the most dominant group, East Indian, European, Chinese, Lebanese, Syrian, and Mayan, and groups with mixed ethnicity such as Mestizo, Mulatto and Creole. The islands of Barbados, St Lucia and Dominica, the foci of this study, are contained in two groups of islands referred to as the Windward and Leeward Islands. They are relatively small in comparison to some of the larger territories such as Jamaica and the Dominican Republic (Appendix III). The official language of the three countries under study is English, but St Lucia and Dominica have both had a greater French presence in the past and to date a French/Creole patois co-exists as another spoken tongue in both of these societies.

The geographical separation between territories, and the disparities in natural resources, made for great variation in the development of the Caribbean islands and have made them subject to internal imbalances within the region itself. On the other hand the territories have a shared history of colonization and decolonization. Barbados, St Lucia and Dominica are independent territories unlike territories such as Puerto Rico, Guadeloupe and Martinique which are still dependencies with imperialist ties. Their small size and openness to the global economy have made full sovereignty virtually impossible in any of these territories. They remain linked by trade and foreign relations to former colonial masters or through economic ties to new ones both within and without the region.

Despite local cultural differences, because of their similarities, especially those due to colonialism, slavery, indentureship, racism, ongoing emigration, and a social structure blended from a mixture of migrant cultures, the region has evolved as a geographical and social entity which is uniquely Caribbean, a generalization which has often disguised the features specific to the smaller islands. It is necessary here to examine the particular characteristics of each of the surveyed territories.

Barbados

Barbados, largely of coral formation and surrounded by miles of white sand and beaches, is 34 km long and 23 km at its widest point. It is a relatively flat country with a small agricultural sector still dominated by sugar cane. Bridgetown is the principal commercial centre, port and largest town, in which shopping facilities are boosted by duty free concessions. Barbados was settled by the English from the seventeenth century and its political climate has remained relatively stable, as has its currency, the Barbados dollar, which, at present, equals one half of the US dollar. The country has promoted itself as one of the key tourist resorts in the region, and this sector provides a major source of employment for women. This has been facilitated by budgetary incentives from the government for upgrading hotels in the island.

The population of Barbados in 1995 was 257,000. Women accounted for 46 percent of the employed total labour force in 1994, of which 7 percent were in agriculture and 11 percent were in industry. Tourism is Barbados' major growth industry, accounting for 16 percent of jobs. Barbados has one of the highest GNP per capita in the region, being US$6,210 in 1992 [*Caribbean Handbook 1995–96*].

Barbados reported the highest calorie intake for its entire population in the Caribbean (3279) compared to the lowest, Haiti (2013). Barbados also boasts the highest level of literacy among the three countries in this study (90 percent in 1991) compared to St Lucia which had 46 percent in 1991.

The total fertility rate estimated for this society was 1.8 in 1992. Life expectancy at birth was 75.1 in 1990, increasing from 64.3 in 1960. The crude birth rate was 16.0 per thousand of the population, while the crude death rate stood at 9.1 in 1992. Contraceptive prevalency was measured at 55 percent between 1986 and 1993 compared to 47 percent in St Lucia and 50 percent in Dominica for the same time period [*Country Human Development Indicators, UNDP, NY, 1993*].

Status of Women in Barbados

Barbados and Dominica reported the highest life expectancy for women in the Caribbean, with Barbados also reporting the highest for men as well – 77 years. 43.5 percent of the population in Barbados are reported to be female heads of households [ECLAC Report 13/9/94]. A CARICOM report on the status of women in sixteen Commonwealth Caribbean countries [Mondesire & Dunn 1995] noted Barbados as having the second highest percentage of female headed households in 1995.

A National Insurance and Social Security Scheme was introduced in 1967 which provides contributory benefits to the employed and self-employed in respect of sickness, maternity and in other areas from which women clearly benefit.

Rosalind Lynch writes that unemployment has generally been a major problem for the island, and that within fluctuations which vary from year to year, female unemployment has always exceeded that of males. In 1980, the male unemployment rate was 9.2 percent, while the female rate was 16.7 percent. The 1995 CARICOM report cited above observed that a high rate of female unemployment (26 percent) now exists in Barbados, because of the closure of several manufacturing firms that employed largely females. Lynch points out that a high level of unemployment among women exists despite the educational opportunities and achievements of women [Lynch 1995]. She argues that at present, women outnumber men in the educational institutions particularly at the secondary level, but not necessarily at the level of tertiary education. Secondary education is provided in 22 government secondary schools, government-aided independent schools and fully independent schools. Cavehill, Barbados is the site of one of three campuses of the UWI, the other two are located in Trinidad and Jamaica. The government pays the fees of all Barbadians attending the University of the West Indies, and the Barbados Community College offers courses in the Liberal Arts, Science, Commerce, Fine Arts, Health Sciences, Hospitality Studies and Technology. Teacher Training is provided by Erdiston Teachers' Training College.

Women in Barbados have had access to progressive legislation since the 1970s including legislation prohibiting violence against women. Barbados was also the second country in the Commonwealth Caribbean to begin providing crisis centres for crimes of sexual abuse. In Barbados prevention programmes have been instituted by the police, including instruction on how to handle cases of sexual assault. In 1983-84 the Medical Termination of Pregnancy Act was passed making abortions legal in this country on specific grounds.

The majority of Barbadian women are Anglican although some other denominations such as Methodist, Moravian and Roman Catholic faiths are represented.

St Lucia

St Lucia was settled by Europeans as a plantation economy and from the eighteenth century the island was at the centre of the struggles between the French and the British, changing hands fourteen times between the two nations. Eventually a British territory, a strong French presence still persists. St Lucia has a fertile and verdant flora and there are many natural attractions such as the twin Pitons or volcanic peaks, mineral baths, lush rain forest as well as pleasant beaches. The island is largely mountainous having an exceedingly rugged interior topography. In St Lucia, agricultural land has become a scarce commodity, farm plots have been subdivided into even smaller parcels and without gainful employment in non-agricultural sectors, people continue to deforest the island to make a living. Nonetheless, agriculture continues to be the island's major economic sector. Its contribution to GDP has, however, declined by half since 1962 from 34 percent to 17 percent in 1986.

The contribution of tourism to GDP during 1962 and 1986 increased from 6.7 percent to 17.1 percent. Other sectors which also increased during this period were export manufacturing (textiles, clothing, beverages, paper and wood products, fabricated metals, electronics), government and local services, but increases in these sectors were not as dramatic.

Castries, the capital city, is the major commercial centre and port. There are two airports, one in Castries for interisland and some international flights, and one on the other side of the island, Vieuxfort, which serves international flights. In less than a generation St Lucia has been transformed from a predominantly rural society to a modern economy with a diversified export base. Low regional wages, investment incentives and the abundance of natural recreational and scenic assets provide the basis for this restructuring. St Lucia today is considered one of the most balanced economies among the smaller islands of the Lesser Antilles. Along with Barbados and Antigua, St Lucia has one of the most developed tourism sectors in the region.

The population of St Lucia was 151,300 in 1995. There has been a decline in the total fertility rate in St Lucia since the 1960s from an average of 6.7 to 3.1 live births per woman in 1991. The age group with the highest fertility rate is 20 to 24. Births to women between 15 and 19 have declined from a high in 1980 of almost 30 percent to 20 percent in 1991. Rapid improvements in health, the fight against communicable diseases, improvements in the public health facilities, cleaner water supply and improved public education have contributed to lower death rates in the past 20 to 25 years. The death rate declined from 14.6 in 1960 to 6.3 per 1000 population in 1991.

Between the period 1970 to 1980 the estimated migration was 1900 persons per year. While out-migration is significant, population and labour force growth has outstripped the economy's capacity to create jobs. As a consequence, island unemployment rose from 14 percent in 1975 to a figure of around 20 percent in the mid 1980s [St Lucia, Country Environment Profile 1991].

Status of Women in St Lucia

Women comprise 52 percent of the population in St Lucia. In 1980 38.8 percent of all households on the island were headed by women; by 1991 this had increased to 40.4 percent. Male unemployment dropped from 15.7 percent to 11.7 percent between 1980 and 1993 while female unemployment rose from 19.2 percent to 22.5 percent for the same period. Total fertility rate moved from 3.8 in 1980 to 3.1 in 1991. Contraceptive prevalence was recorded in 1988 as being 58 percent. Teenage pregnancy is a problem as the rate of births to women in the 15–19 age group, though declining, is still unacceptably high.

One area of development in the last two decades has been in the availability of tertiary education in St Lucia provided by the Sir Arthur Lewis Community College, which offers first year university education to nationals. At tertiary level, girls have moved from 47 percent to 64 percent between 1985 and 1991.

Of particular benefit to women in the last decade have been initiatives emerging from the first international conference on women during International Women's Year in 1975 and the Nairobi Conference in 1985. Achievements include the establishment of government machinery for the advancement of women in 1986, the adoption of a National Policy in 1991, the establishment of a Crisis Centre to deal with issues of domestic violence, the proliferation of community based women's groups, 'Mother's and Father's Groups', and other programmes on gender sensitization.

The National Report on the Status of Women in St Lucia, prepared for the United Nations Fourth World Conference in Beijing, noted that there were at present 40 women's organizations and groups in the island. The groups' activities involve mainly community services and family life education. There are a further 70 'Mothers' and 'Fathers' groups, the majority of which are located in the rural districts. Other women's organizations include the National Council of Women's Voluntary Organizations, the Women's Caucuses of the National Youth Council and the trade unions, and the women's arms of the two main political parties.

Research has revealed that women are close to achieving a 50 percent representation in the Upper House/Senate. Women's representation in the judicial system increased substantially from 13 percent in 1980 to 39 percent in 1993 largely due to the huge increase in the numbers of women entering the legal profession as attorneys at law. Improvements in women's participation in the decision-making process in the business sector may be seen through the 10 percent increase from 21 percent to 31 percent of women employers with paid staff, and the 7 percent increase from 29 percent to 36 percent in women who were self employed but did not have any paid staff.

Providing day care and preschool services is one method by which the government has helped to ease the burden of working mothers. The Roman Catholic Church and the St Lucia Crisis Centre improve legal awareness for women and provide legal assistance through a Legal Aid Clinic. In St Lucia laws to address domestic violence are being drafted.

Some key areas of concern which still need to be addressed include: equal opportunity in employment, equality for spouses in the acquisition of citizenship, the recognition of common-law spouses' inheritance rights, sexual harassment and the abolition of illegitimate status. Female teachers are discriminated against as they are dismissed if still unwed by the time their second child is born in St Lucia [*National Report on the Status of Women*, 1994].

Dominica

Dominica is the largest of the Windward Islands and lies between the French islands of Guadeloupe and Martinique. It has a total area of 790 square kilometres, supporting dense tropical forests which are uninhabitable. The island is volcanic in origin, the landscape is dominated by high mountains covered with rich tropical forests, and numerous freshwater rivers. The rugged landscape, rising in some places to heights of near 1380 metres, means that settlement is principally along the coast. Abundant rainfall of up to 200 centimetres a year, coupled with difficult terrain, has hindered the development of large scale plantations, although there has been the commercial production of bananas, which dominates the economy, and food production for household use and the domestic market is carried on in the island.

The high level of rainfall in this country has resulted in close to 365 flowing rivers, a feature which causes the island to be referred to as "The Land of Many Rivers". This geography gives Dominica a uniqueness in that it has adverse effects on the communication system and on the extent to which "economic development" can penetrate the interior. On the other hand, Dominica has not developed as a conventional tourist destination, but has acquired instead a reputation among a more select group of nature lovers and those interested in mountain and forest vacations, rather than the wide popularity of beach vacations marketed by the other two islands.

The population of Dominica is 71,800 (1995), and its capital city Roseau has a population of 20,000 residents while the other chief town, Portsmouth has 8,000. Unlike the capital cities of Barbados and St Lucia, Roseau displays a facade of traditional wooden buildings (see Profiles).

Dominica's history, like that of St Lucia, is also a mixture of colonialisms. French settlers entered Dominica at the end of the seventeenth century, but the island was ceded to Britain in 1763. Thus the population consists of largely

Afro-Caribbean English- and French patois-speaking inhabitants and about 700 Caribs who remain in a small reserve on the windward coast. The Caribs are descendants of the indigenous Amerindian population of the Caribbean region which was largely decimated by Spanish colonization. The remaining Caribs intermarried with African maroons to produce a Black Carib population, small groups of which still exist in Dominica, St Vincent and Belize.

In 1995, the economy was still based mainly on the banana industry. More recently, agricultural diversification, development of light industry and greater emphasis on tourism are being given attention. Agriculture is closely tied with a growing eco-tourism sector. Virtually all the tourist spots are in farming areas and the excellent feeder network provides access to visitors, which itself allows increased possibilities for "on farm" sales. Much of the diversification in terms of vegetable and flower production has also been geared towards the hotels and restaurants [*The Courier* No. 140, 1993]. Unemployment was estimated at just below 15 percent in 1994.

Education is free and is compulsory for those between five and 15. In addition to nursery education, there are 65 primary and 13 secondary schools, as well as a community college with technical and academic divisions and a teacher training college. The adult literacy rate is estimated at 90 percent.

Status of Women in Dominica

Women comprise 50.2 percent of the population in Dominica. The proportion of household heads who are female is estimated at 38 percent. Average household size is five persons and the majority of households (59.8 percent) had between three to six persons. There are more families with both parents in the home (39.5 percent) than single parent families (25.3 percent).[1]

Fertility data for 1990 show live births per thousand women, age 15–44 years, to be 83 with over 50 percent of the births occurring between the ages of 23 to 29. The largest number of births occur to women holding visiting union status. The low number of births occurring during marriage (20 percent) is associated with the phenomenon that for many couples marriage most often takes place after childbearing is completed. In general legal marriage prevailed over common-law and single status.

As a result of the 1986 Structural Adjustment Programme which led to major cutbacks in social services expenditure, general unemployment rose to 14 percent, with unemployment among women being higher at 22.4 percent. This has exacerbated emigration and led to the drain of professionals. Women are still heavily concentrated in agriculture although this has ceased to be a major employer of women regionally as a result of the increasing mechaniza-

---

[1]These figures, taken from the *Report on the Status of Women in the Commonwealth of Dominica* (1994), are based on a survey carried out with a sample of 1912 women. The percentages do not add up to 100 as the other respondents may have been single women who had not started their own families.

tion of labour intensive tasks. Manufacturing declined about 2 percent in 1991 as a result of marketing problems and agroprocessing competition from synthetics. There has been a growth in the industrial sector of assembly and small industries such as canning of fruit pieces, meat processing, dairy products, vanilla extraction, soft drinks and timber products. Other local industries include handicrafts and, more recently, jewellery. All of these industries have benefitted women by providing employment opportunities.

Dominica has addressed educational improvement by upgrading some primary schools to secondary level, amalgamating at the community college level, supporting technical/vocational training, establishing school feeding programmes and providing preschool education programmes as well as inservice teacher training programmes. Despite these changes, the country still experiences a shortage of schools, educational supplies, teaching aids and qualified teachers. Government statistics showed that 55 percent of all primary school teachers and 75 percent of all secondary school teachers were not fully certified. Government statistics for 1991 point out that more males completed primary level while women ranked higher in completion of secondary education. Women were slightly better educated than men at pre-university/post secondary levels, while men exceeded women in completion of university degrees. The proportion of adults with vocational training represents a higher percentage of males as compared to females in 1991.

Unlike in Barbados and St Lucia, women who seek legal redress for violations of property and inheritance and maintenance rights, for criminal acts, violence and domestic abuse, have access to a range of legislation. Among the legislation available to the women of Dominica are the Married Woman's Property Ordinance, the Matrimonial Clauses Act, 1973 and the Children and Young Persons Act, 1970. The most recent changes in legislation are to be found in the Maintenance Act, 1981, and the Age of Majority Act, 1983. There are no developments in the legislation regarding abortion, which remains illegal, nor in areas pertaining to sexual violence, other than existing criminality laws.

There has been an increase in women's participation in top level public service positions such as permanent secretaries, magistrates, principals of secondary schools as well as medical officers. There is also a post of Co-ordinator of Women's Affairs in the public service. The Status of Women Report of the Dominica National Council on Women [1995] noted, however, that "this visible achievement of successful women masks the reality of those who are unable to break out of the cycle of childbearing, unstable relationships with men and endless poverty. It is evident that the majority of women labour long hours both inside and outside the home, tolerating incredible uncertainties. The general stereotype of a Dominican woman is a strong matriarch. Yet hypertension is so common, it is taken for granted."

Migration

Migration is a key element in the history of the Caribbean and particularly so in the continuous development of the three societies under scrutiny. The earlier historical waves of migration and settlement of the three societies differed though and this has made for differences in the opportunities and outlook of the people who inhabit the islands. For instance St Lucia still has its French influence through the patois spoken on the island, while Barbados has been completely anglicized since the settlement of this island. Because of its proximity to Guadeloupe and Martinique and the French influence on the island of Dominica itself, the French islands have attracted some level of ongoing migration from Dominica.

While the postemancipation and nineteenth century movements clearly also involved women, it is useful here to focus on the features of the twentieth century migration trends. During the decades of the 1950s and 1960s outward migration flow from the Caribbean was male dominated, but this trend was reversed in the decades of the 1970s and 1980s when there was an exodus of women ranging from domestic and industrial workers to health professionals and teachers all seeking employment out of the country. It is reported that the net migration for women was over 50 percent higher than that of men from the second half of the twentieth century.

The outward migration of women from the Caribbean region as well as internal shifts between rural and urban districts, and between Caribbean territories, have been examined by many researchers. In a study which focused on the islands of St Kitts and Nevis, Margaret Byron draws attention to some of the features which were common to all of the smaller territories in the region which were less equipped than the larger ones to cope with shifts in the economic mode of production from plantations and estates, to commercial and industrial ventures. She points out that the small densely populated islands of the Eastern Caribbean became a source of labour in the late nineteenth century, and a reserve army of labour for United States and multinational investments in these territories. Various movements in the late nineteenth and early twentieth centuries can be charted from Barbados to Venezuela, from Dominica to Trinidad, and from the three societies of Barbados, Dominica and St Lucia to Central America, the Dominican Republic and later to the United Kingdom and the United States. Byron notes that "a feature of this dependence on occupation opportunities abroad, was the redirection of the migrant flow when social and economic conditions at a particular destination rendered British West Indian labour an unnecessary part of production" [Byron 1994: 35]. These migrations were in general meant to be of a temporary nature, and men moved with the idea of remitting funds to their families at home, while women remained at home to manage households and the provision lands. In this respect Byron concludes that the impact of migration was much greater in the smaller islands; for example, the male-female ratio in Jamaica remained more stable and balanced than that of Barbados. St Lucia also suffered a similar fate to that of Barbados in this migration movement.

Figures available but not disaggregated by sex related to the migration moves which would directly begin to affect the lives of our respondents in this study indicated that between 1955 and 1961, 18,741 persons from Barbados migrated to Britain and 7,291 migrated from St Lucia. In-depth studies of these movements suggest that while there was a predominance of men, this movement began to attract families, including families comprised of women and their children [Byron 1994]. Byron again points to some of the features of this movement for migrants' aspirations.

The consequent period of settlement in Britain has been accompanied by family extension and a gradual familiarization with a British, urban way of life. This familiarity and close British network of offspring and relatives and friends from a variety of origins has led many migrants to reconsider their initial commitment to returning to reside in the Caribbean. In many cases, such doubts have been fuelled by migrant's convictions that they have not accumulated the capital to enable them to make a 'prosperous' return [Byron 1994: 199].

A crucial element in the examination of this shift in migration is the human agency which affected decision making of individuals. While the Caribbean had in general been viewed first as a settlement of groups of migrants for plantation labour, and second as a source of seasonal and temporary labour supply for development projects in other parts of the western hemisphere, the later movements signalled changes in migrants' perceptions of themselves and their rights to property, additional occupational roles and opportunities for education and jobs for their children born in these new territories. Into this shifting perception of migration we must place women's aspirations to migrate: in order to improve their career choices, and to provide for their families, regardless of a male presence. If opportunities such as education were not available in their home territories, then migration represented an alternative. The new options for migration as we enter the last quarter of the twentieth century were not restricted to Britain, but included a movement to the United States, and to other Caribbean territories which appeared to offer more possibilities for self-improvement. For instance within the Caribbean, Barbados is viewed as offering greater opportunities for education and employment by women of St Lucia and Dominica.

In this study we focus on women's perceptions of what migration promises, and the purposes for which migration is used. In the meantime, the subtle shift which is simultaneously occurring in the popular understanding of migration must be incorporated. While migration appeared to offer the goals of occupation, some monetary satisfaction and the acquisition of a more worldly view of life, the stories of returning migrants or the dissatisfaction created by loss of national and cultural identities, family ties, old friends and familiar spaces, have reverberated a competing ideology. For some Caribbean migrants, personal and individual goals cannot be fully realized in a foreign land, replete with its own internal dynamics which largely exclude or marginalize the migrant. The politicization of peoples in the region about their national identities and their cultural specificities has led to new ways of seeing migration. Women, who have been central in these later streams, have been equally part of this new definition of Caribbean identity as it is framed in relation to the "developed" world.

A contemporary consideration of migration needs to assess the aspirations of migrants to return, even when they do not do so, and to identify the numbers who have deliberately chosen to migrate temporarily for reasons of education and experience abroad, and have subsequently returned to work in their territories.

Analysis of Data From Questionnaire

Preliminaries

The primary data collected from the responses of the women who were part of the questionnaire survey are analysed in this chapter along with the insights gleaned from the collection of in-depth oral histories.

The largest proportion of the respondents in this survey were concentrated in the 20–24 and 25–29 age groups with a smaller number of respondents drawn from the 15–19, 30–34 and 35–39 age groups. From the table it is clear that the majority of the interviewees were still young. They were likely to be among those women taking decisions which could lead to fundamental change in their lives, as for instance decisions to have children or migrate, or to opt for educational opportunities and a career instead of marriage. The respondents were also born in the latter half of the twentieth century. Those in the over 40 age group, representing 10 percent of the sample in all three territories, are women who have completed fertility. This gives us the chance to look at a longer cycle of decision making in a woman's life. In general the sample interviewed represented women of childbearing age in the three societies.

Table 1: Age of Respondents in Sample

	15–19	20–24	25–29	30–34	35–39	40–44	Over 44	No Response	Total
Barbados	19	26	22	23	19	13	-	3	125
St Lucia	16	34	29	19	15	7	5	-	125
Dominica	18	31	27	18	17	10	2	2	125

Parents' History

In general, as individual women and men, we have all been influenced, to a greater or lesser extent, by the life chances, class position and experiences of our parents. The preliminary information gathered in both the questionnaire and in the oral history interviews attempts to understand the opportunities which women were given by their parents, as well as to investigate the way in which their own ideas of relationships and the need for individual decisions regarding self development were informed by the marital status and life experiences of their mothers and fathers.

The choices which the respondents have made with respect to their lives and those of their children were dependent on such factors as the presence or absence of both parents or of a single parent in their own upbringing, the conjugal status of the mother, the kind of relationship between the parents, whether parents have lived together or maintained separate households, the number of siblings they had and the opportunities they were allowed, and the quality of life they saw their parents enjoy. In addition many parents held traditional views of the roles and future of their male and female offspring, with the boys being socialized for the workplace and the girls for bearing children and getting married.

The proportion of parents in the sample of respondents who were legally married was 48 percent for Barbados, 47 percent for St Lucia and 32 percent for Dominica. There was some ambiguity among the respondents in reporting whether parents were in common-law marriages. This could account perhaps for the low number who reported that their parents had common-law unions, being six in Barbados, three in St Lucia and two[1] in Dominica (Table 2). The WICP data had found that 11 percent of the sample of 594 women interviewed for this project were currently in common-law unions. This would suggest that the other category of responses which were cited as not married but did not specify the type of union could also be grouped under the common-law status. If these two categories are grouped, then the number of parents in common-law unions would be 7 percent for Barbados, 16 percent for St Lucia and 17 percent for Dominica. An interesting response for parents' marital history was the number who stated that both or one of their parents were married, but in partnerships other than the one into which the respondent was born. The number of cases where both parents were now married to other partners was two in Barbados, seven in St Lucia and two for Dominica. The number of cases where the father was married but to someone other than the mother at the time of the respondent's birth, was 15 for Barbados, 11 for St Lucia and 19 for Dominica. Obversely, responses that the mother was married and the

---

[1]Where numbers are included in the text this refers to the actual number of respondents in the sample who gave their responses. The sample was a relatively small one and percentages are sometimes unrevealing.

Table 2:   Marital Status of Parents of Respondents

Marital Status	Barbados	St Lucia	Dominica
Married together	61	59	41
Common-law	6	3	2
Both married to other partners	2	7	2
Not married (did not state whether common-law or other type of union)	3	17	19
Not married and not together	11	8	15
Father married/mother not married	15	11	19
Mother married/father not married	2	4	5
Mother married/don't know father	2	3	–
Separated/divorced	15	5	5
Don't know	1	1	1
No response	7	7	16
TOTAL	125	125	125

father was not were significantly lower, being two for Barbados, four for St Lucia and five for Dominica.

A significant difference between the three societies was the higher number of divorces or separations among respondents' parents in Barbados – this being 15, compared to five for both St Lucia and Dominica. Two factors which may account for this difference are, first, the higher legally married rates in Barbados thus leading to higher legal separations, and second, the difference in religious affiliations between the societies, with Barbados being predominantly Anglican, and St Lucia and Dominica being predominantly Roman Catholic.

It is useful to examine the distribution of parents' occupations before we move on later to the occupations chosen by respondents themselves. The occupations in which mothers were most found in Barbados were domestic helpers, messengers and janitors, shop attendants, hotel workers, cooks and clothes vendors, housewives, 23; and professionals and semi-professionals including teachers, nurses and nursing aids, civil servant, secretary, 28. Six mothers worked as agricultural labourers while the rest were distributed evenly among such self-employed occupations as shopkeeping, floristry and landscape artist. The most prominent occupation in which mothers were listed in St Lucia was farming and agriculture related industry, 35; the second highest occurring occupation was housewifery with 22; and professional and semi-professional occupations including postmistress, secretary, manager, civil servant, clerk, security guard and hotel worker, accounted for nine mothers. The self-employed category, 13 in number, comprised small shop owners, hairdressers, seamstresses, and one masseuse. In Dominica the category of mothers listed as housewives was the largest, being 39, followed by farming and farm related activities such as vending and huckstering which accounted for 38 mothers. The professional and semi-professional category which included teaching, nursing, NGO worker, clerical, and civil servant held 12 women. The self-employed category including a small shopkeeper, caterer, baker and seamstress had eight women.

Fathers' occupations in Barbados were concentrated among professionals including architects, engineers, lawyers, doctors, civil servants and managers with 31, and tradesmen which accounted for 15. Ten fathers were listed as involved in farming and farm related activities, while four fathers were listed as unemployed. Farming and farm-related activities were predominant among fathers in St Lucia, the number involved in these activities being thirty five. Ten fathers were employed in professional occupations including a civil servant, supervisor, pastor, manager and policemen. Thirty-three fathers were employed in service industries and trade, including firemen, taxi-drivers and builders. There were five self-employed while one was cited as being unemployed. The largest category of occupations in which fathers were found in Dominica was farming and fishing with 38, followed by 16 in trades and service industries. The professional and semi-professional category including clerical, civil servant and pharmacist and health officer held 15 fathers. Six fathers were self-employed and one was unemployed.

Of the total sample of women, 57 parents in Barbados had all their children together, either in legal or common-law unions, while 51 parents in St Lucia and 29 in Dominica had children together. The most pertinent feature which emerged when we examined the number of siblings which respondents had, was the wide variation in family sizes. Family size varied between one and 24, the latter comprising offspring from separate families of two parents of the respondents. The average family size which respondents came from varied from six children per family in Barbados, eleven children in St Lucia and eight children in Dominica.

Education

Of the three territories surveyed, Barbados is the island which boasts the highest standard of "development" and is also the site of one of the three campuses of the University of the West Indies. St Lucia has a vibrant community college, the Sir Arthur Lewis Community College, a department of continuing studies of the University of the West Indies, and Dominica also has a community college.

Table 3:   Educational Level of Respondents in Sample

	Primary	Senior primary/ pre-secondary	Completed & pursuing secondary	Secondary(tech/voc/ secretarial)	Incomplete secondary	Tertiary(community coll., technical, nursing)	Pursuing tertiary (community coll.)	Completed & pursuing tertiary university	Pursuing adult education	Total
Barbados	9	-	41	-	7	15	4	49	-	125
St Lucia	43	21	26	7	14	13	-	1	-	125
Dominica	60	1	36	3	9	13	-	2	1	125

The first part of this discussion covers the responses to questions (2) to (5) under section B: Education, of the questionnaire. While we need to allow for some randomness in the choice of survey participants, the level of education attained by the women in the various societies is consistent with the development of the education system in each society. At 49 or 39.2 percent of the sample, Barbados shows the highest level of persons who have attained tertiary education at university and community college. Fifteen or 12 percent of the sample in Barbados also had technical and nursing qualifications.

The majority of the interviewees in Dominica had attained only primary level education (48 percent) as compared to St Lucia where 34.4 percent of the interviewees had had primary level education, and Barbados where 7.2 percent admitted to only primary level education. A similar proportion had had access to, or were at the time pursuing, secondary level education, between 25 percent and 30 percent for each of the islands (Table 3). This data tallies with general statistics of educational attainment in the three societies.

A crucial point of concern in the interview was the numbers and percentages of those who indicated an incomplete secondary education, and the negligible number who stated that they were pursuing adult education. It is useful to examine some of the reasons why girls stopped education at primary level, why secondary education could not be completed and why few women were able to move on to adult education.

Four of the 125 women in Barbados who responded to this question (Question 5, Appendix 1) said that they had stopped school because of pregnancy. Nine women said they had not been successful at the common entrance examinations and had reached the age to stop primary school. One divulged that her mother was an alcoholic and embarrassed her at school, and one admitted that her parents were poor and could not afford to send her.

In St Lucia the responses were equally explicit as to the reasons why girls had either chosen or had been unable to pursue secondary or higher education. Four respondents admitted they had stopped because of pregnancies, 22 respondents said they had reached the age to stop school, of whom five had already completed primary school, six said that they had not passed the common entrance examinations to move on. While five said their mothers could not send them to school, eight gave the reason as financial problems, indicating perhaps that the financial decisions in the former case were made by the mother rather than being a joint parental decision. In one case the parents decided that the girl must stop school because she had started teaching at age fourteen. Less frequently given reasons for leaving school were the following: "brother wanted me to babysit for him"; "to take care of younger children"; "because of involvement with my boyfriend"; "tired of going to school"; and "health problems". While the importance of schooling for girls has been firmly established in the Caribbean, certainly over the last five decades, the responses indicate that in some cases the education of young girls is still being viewed as secondary to the demands of the wider family.

In Dominica, five women said they left school because of pregnancies, 46 or 36.8 percent of the sample said they had left school because they reached the age of fifteen, of whom 21 said they had not passed the common entrance examinations. Two respondents said they had begun teaching, one at the age of 14 and the other got a job as a teacher in a secondary school. Schooling itself presented a problem for some of the women; one admitted to a misunderstanding with a teacher, one indicated that she was disappointed in her chosen subject of typing at the vocational level, another that she was not learning anything, and yet another that she did not like school.

Financial difficulties clearly prevented a number of the respondents in Dominica from moving on to higher education. Here were some of the reasons which cover both the financial concerns of educating girls as well as the attitudes to further education for women: "sister took me out to look after her children"; "take care of siblings"; "taken to Roseau to look after children"; "domestic problems"; "couldn't get along with my mother"; "father not supportive and mother couldn't afford to"; and "mother took me out". Two respondents also indicated different reasons why girls would choose to leave school – one admitted to being overweight and not being able to cope with this. The other was suspended for eating in class and did not return.

Questions (6) and (7) asked respondents if they would have liked to continue education and, if so, why? These incorporated both those who had had minimal education up to primary level and those who had proceeded beyond primary level and would have liked to have advanced further. Since 109 women in the sample in Barbados had actually achieved secondary and tertiary level education, this question yielded no response in many cases here. The responses in St Lucia where 78 women had achieved up to primary level education ranged as follows: "to get a better job"; "to learn a trade"; "for self development and because I would have liked to be educated". In Dominica,

70 women achieved up to primary level education and gave these kinds of responses: "Oh yes, without a good education today you are nowhere"; "for a better future"; "yes I wanted to move on in life and achieve something"; "yes so I could have had a good job"; "today, education is all – a home, a job, a good life." These findings suggest that whereas for women in Barbados the access to education may be a taken-for-granted privilege, in St Lucia and especially in Dominica, education is additionally perceived as the means to a better quality of life.

Career History

The questions in this section require a qualitative overview rather than primarily a quantitative analysis. This is so because the questionnaire pursued a chronology as well as explanations for shifts in respondents' careers. In addition the section also attempted to assess the value of work outside of the home to women.

We investigated whether or not the sample of women actually had choices in terms of a career or occupation, or whether the circumstances of their lives, be they economic, social or personal, militated against any real choices on their part. In addition, in this section we sought to understand whether having a career made a difference to women either in terms of a definition of self, or the contribution it made to their economic well being, and thus to the power they possessed to change unsatisfactory living conditions. In other words, do Caribbean women from these islands make conscious decisions about career, or is it a sphere of life in which choices are few, limited or very rarely available?

Barbados

The list of occupations cited as first job held by the respondents is very broad but provides a good indication of the way in which women begin their employment outside of the home. Of the 125 respondents in Barbados, nine women stated they had no career. This figure included one who said that her first and only job was that of a medical records clerk as a temporary summer position. One woman did not respond to this section of the questionnaire. The rest of the sample were all employed at some point although at the time of the interview 10 women actually stated that they were unemployed. The lack of response to present employment in several cases, and the movement to self-employment in many others, support an ongoing theory about female unemployment in the labour force – that this is more disguised than male unemployment figures.

In the entire sample, only one woman stated that she had made a decision to stop working as ceramist to become a wife and mother. In three instances, the women stated openly that their first and present job was that of home-maker; at home taking care of baby, and, at home looking after her child. In some other cases where this may have applied, ie, that women were also wives and mothers, the women themselves did not recognize that this also represented work.

White collar jobs were cited as the largest source for first occupations. These included clerical officers in government service, trainee accountants and accounts clerks, bookkeepers, cashiers, sales clerks, bank tellers, secretaries, typists, receptionists, office attendants, trainees in customer relations, advertising accounts representatives, primary school teachers, art teachers, Christian education officer, social worker, camp counsellor and library assistants. They comprised 66 percent of the sample. Machine operators, seamstresses, waitresses, entertainers, defence force recruits (2); day care assistant, nursing assistant, basket maker and craftswoman, model, weather presenter, worker in tourism made up another 18 percent of the sample. Two respondents said that their first job was that of babysitting while three started as domestic helpers. Of the jobs chosen by this group of women, few are deemed non-traditional ones according to the prevalent sexual division of labour: among these would be the defence force jobs and a landscaper's assistant.

With respect to present employment of women in the sample, the largest category was that of professionals which included lawyer, consultant, manager, teacher, nurse, social worker and guidance officer. Clerical workers accounted for 15 percent of the sample: these comprised accounts clerks, bank tellers, data entry operators, and typists. The remaining categories included six self-employed women, five housewives, seven domestic workers and other individual occupations such as waitresses, craftworkers, factory workers and machine operators. Twelve women were not working because they were still in school and 11 were unemployed at the time of the interview.

Only 13 percent of women started with the same job which they were doing at the time of the interview. Of those who had shifted jobs, this was done for self improvement or for reasons which included: to get more money, to experience different challenges in life, more flexibility to be with new baby, promotion, health problems, dismissed wrongfully, sexual harassment, frustration, opportunity to learn more about area of interest, better work environment, and to become better qualified. There was also an increase in status and salary between the first job and the present jobs women held. Many women continued or entered further studies or training between their first and present jobs.

Question 19 under this category of career history asked women if they thought work was important to a woman and if so why. In general most women responded in the affirmative and cited independence from their parents, spouses or partners, ability to support children and to build self-confidence and self-esteem as reasons for the value of work. The following responses represent the sentiments of the majority.

Work is important so that women can gain an income, they do not have to be dependent on spouses or anyone. It allows for some degree of independence.

Yes, work is important to a woman for personal satisfaction and it gives her a sense of empowerment.

Yes, work is important to a woman. It gives you a sense of independence, gives a feeling of self esteem but I have no problem with being a housewife, it's my individual personal choice.

St Lucia

Of the 125 respondents in St Lucia, a career history could not be followed for two women who were still at school. Seven women were unemployed at the time of the interview due to being laid off or pressure at work, and for other unstated reasons. Unemployment was itself a choice for some women as an interim measure to seeking better jobs. The rest of the women in the sample were all gainfully occupied and many had changed jobs at some point. Thirty-five of the women had clerical positions as their first jobs, in occupations such as data entry clerk, receptionist, accounts clerk, sales clerk and typist. Nineteen women worked as domestics or babysitters at homes or in hotels, 17 began as teachers, three were housewives and one was a self-employed seamstress. The first occupation for other women in the sample included being waitresses, factory workers, machine operators and workers in craft centres.

At the time of the survey the number of women employed in clerical, domestic and professional occupations had decreased. The number of housewives had increased to eight and the self-employed category had increased to four. The three women who became self-employed entered shopkeeping.

Among the reasons cited for changing jobs (Question 14) in St Lucia were for better salary and more opportunities; sexual harassment; internal migration; had children out of wedlock; mother was sick and had to help on the farm; too much manual labour; wanted to be independent; job security; and to become better qualified. The career history of women in St Lucia points to some degree of mobility for women, but at the same time toward a limit of opportunities for career development within the society.

With regard to the importance of work to women in St Lucia, as in Barbados, the majority of women said that work was important to them and, they felt, to women in general. It is interesting that in this society women link work to facilitating independence, either as ownership of property or having their own "pay packet", but several also indicated that it was important to help a partner. There were very aggressive stances taken regarding the independence which came from working, as stated by one woman, "Of course, every woman should be able to maintain their own selves; stand on their own two feet, and, dominate their life."

Dominica

In Dominica, 13 women were still in school and therefore career history could not be followed for these. As in St Lucia and Barbados, clerical jobs were the most popular as the first jobs which women had, accounting for 38 first jobs in this society. Twenty-five women had first jobs which were either in baby sitting or some related domestic activity, eight were in professional areas of either teaching or nursing, five were housewives and none of the women stated self-employment as their first occupation. Among the others who had worked, their first jobs included road cleaning, cooking, or being waitresses, factory workers, produce packers and syrup bottlers. At the time of the survey there was a decrease in the total number of women employed in clerical work, 20, and six in domestic occupations. There was, however, an increase in professional to 14, which in addition to teaching and nursing now included NGO coordinator and dental therapist. The number of housewives had increased to seventeen. Eight women decided after their first jobs to become self-employed as hairdressers, craftmakers and seamstresses. Eleven women of the sample were now unemployed.

Some of the reasons which women gave for changing jobs were: "it was a temporary job"; "I was not satisfied and wanted to work for myself"; "for more scope and better pay"; "pregnancy"; "the woman I worked for was not nice"; and "had to leave teaching because of pregnancy".

The responses in Dominica with respect to Question 19 (Do you think work is important to women and if so why?) were again very similar to those given in St Lucia and Barbados. Most women stated "yes" to whether or not work was important to women, and were emphatic about this in most instances. Again, it was about the independence which work gave them from partners and the capacity to provide for themselves and their children. Some of the responses from women to this question were also very revealing about the nature of gender relations in this society:

So that they can be independent. It is not the best thing to sit and wait for men to give them money.

Yes, because she does not have to depend solely on someone else for everything and according to the kind of partner she has, makes her feel like a beggar.

Absolutely, it gives her a chance to feel good about herself and be a role model for her daughter.

Oh yes, I experience when my mother was not working how hard life was for us.

Yes, it gives the opportunities to direct my life, instead of others directing life for me.

Referring back to parents' occupation we can note that a shift has taken place between mother's occupation and the occupation women engage in today. For Barbados, 23 mothers were employed as housewives compared to five of the respondents today; there were 22 housewives and 30 farmers listed among mother's occupations in St Lucia and the present occupational distribution of daughters today in St Lucia showed eight housewives and five farmers. Among mothers there were 30 farmers and 39 housewives in Dominica, whereas among the respondents there were 17 housewives and three farmers.

Migration History

Migration has for a long time in the history of the region represented a way in which peoples of the Caribbean have sought tertiary or vocational education, more occupational choices if not actual employment, and a shift from the provinciality which a relatively small society breeds. These possibilities were for a long time, until the 1950s, the prerogative of men. Figures for migration before 1950 show for instance that male outmigration historically outstripped female migration. In the region the smaller societies have systematically been drained of their population resource with both extraregional and regional destinations being receivers of migrants. Within societies, there have always been internal rural/urban shifts but these movements have generally accelerated in the second half of the twentieth century, as evidenced by increasing urban overflows and inner city slums.

Despite popular notions that migration is an alternative for Caribbean women, in the three islands surveyed the majority of women interviewed indicated that they had never travelled or migrated for reasons of seeking employment, educational advancement or for personal reasons. The proportion of women who had not migrated either internally or externally from their island was 36.0 percent in Barbados compared with 60.8 percent in St Lucia and 52.8 percent in Dominica. Table 4 shows the migration history of the sample of respondents for the three territories. This tendency for migration, especially to countries out of the Caribbean, is particularly striking for Barbados, which shows the highest proportion of women moving out of Barbados, 21.6 percent in this island, as compared to 4.8 percent in St Lucia and 6.4 percent in Dominica.

Questions 21 and 22 in the questionnaire asked women if they felt that opportunities for women would be greater in another Caribbean island or out of the Caribbean and if so why. In general women in Barbados did not perceive

Table 4:   Migration History of Respondents

	Barbados	St Lucia	Dominica
Internal intra-island	37	26	27
Caribbean			
External intra- and extraregional	14	14	23
International	26	6	7
Never migrated	45	76	66
No response	3	3	2
Total	125	125	125

that another Caribbean island would offer them better opportunities since they saw Barbados as one of the more developed Caribbean countries. For those who stated other Caribbean countries as potential destinations, these were Trinidad, Jamaica, Turks and Caicos Islands and the British Virgin Islands. The majority of women in the sample in Barbados however cited that Canada, the United States and the United Kingdom would provide better opportunities for education and employment, and that they would be able to combine work and study in these societies.

Women in St Lucia observed that the other Caribbean countries did not provide alternatives for improved opportunities although 30 respondents cited several countries in the Caribbean where they felt they could get greater access to jobs and education and a better quality of life, these countries being Barbados, St Croix in the US Virgin Islands, Martinique, Trinidad, Puerto Rico and St Maarten. Of those who cited countries out of the Caribbean the popular choices were Canada, the United States and the United Kingdom, for reasons of education, jobs, and better opportunities for self development.

In the case of Dominica a larger number from the sample – 55 – felt that other Caribbean islands offered possibilities for development. Among the Caribbean territories they cited were St Thomas and St Croix in the US Virgin Islands, St Maarten, Antigua, Trinidad, Jamaica, Barbados, Puerto Rico, Martinique, Guadeloupe, St Lucia, St Kitts and Tortola in the British Virgin Islands. The majority of Dominican women felt that opportunities were greater in the United States and Canada, with a limited number citing the United Kingdom as a destination for migration. The reasons given for identifying the USA and Canada included, like those given in Barbados and St Lucia, access to education and jobs.

Barbados

Internal migration in Barbados was rural to rural, but more so rural to suburban and rural to urban. The proportion of women in the sample who migrated internally was 29.6 percent. Of these, many women moved from a rural district to a suburban area, as for instance from St Peter to St James and St Michael (see Appendix III) because their family had moved, to move into their own home with their spouse, and because they had got married to someone who lived in an urban area. Family relationships here referred to marital relationships and marriage, and were the most frequent reasons given for this move. One woman said she moved from a rural to urban district to accommodate her husband's studies and his business. There were no responses about women moving from rural to suburban to facilitate studies although the University of the West Indies, Cave Hill campus is situated in a suburban region. A possible explanation for this might be due to the efficient transportation system in Barbados.

A significant proportion had moved from one rural area to another, as for instance St Lucy to St Peter. Among the responses for those who had moved from rural to rural were: parents moving, family relocation, or to live with her father who had moved away from her mother's residence.

There were a few instances in this society when the movement was urban to rural and here again we find that the reasons for movement were tied up with family decisions. In one instance, her grandmother had died and she went to live in the country with her other grandmother. In another case we see that the woman had moved from a rural area to an urban area to be married but when the marriage broke down she returned to live in the rural area.

St Lucia

Internal migration in St Lucia was, in general, rural to urban as well as rural to rural and in some instances urban to rural. The proportion of women who migrated internally was 20.8 percent. Of these only four women had moved from a rural village to Castries, the main city. The main reasons given for this move were for jobs, and in the case of one woman, to live with a partner and start a family. Vieuxfort in St Lucia may be described as suburban since it is the site of the international airport, and of some tourist activity. It therefore offers opportunities for employment as well. In the case where one woman moved for employment to Vieuxfort, the decision to move was on her own volition.

The larger proportion had actually moved from one rural area to another, as for instance from La Clery to Chase Gardens, Grand Reviere to Gros Islet and Dennery village to Grand Reviere (see Appendix III). To a large extent those who moved from rural to rural were as a result of either of their parents moving, but for one woman it was to live with her father instead of mother, and for another, to move into her husband's residence.

There were several instances when the movement was urban to rural and here again we find that the reasons for movement were linked to family decisions: to live with boyfriend, because parents moved, for the relationship, to babysit for a lady or as in a move from Babonneau to Gros Islet because Babonneau was not good for the children because of drugs. Babonneau which is situated quite close to Castries was also experiencing the overflow of problems created by a growing urban environment, of drugs, lack of employment opportunities and overcrowding.

Dominica

Sixty-six respondents stated that they had not migrated either internally or externally. Twenty-seven migrated internally, mainly from rural to urban Dominica, particularly to Roseau, and the reasons given were job related, for education, to live with their partner, to take care of siblings or live with relatives. Those who migrated from one rural district to the next usually did so to live with relatives or because of a relationship. Twenty-three migrated out of Dominica at some point in their lives. In the majority of cases this was job related. Other reasons include for further education, to join partners and to travel with their parents who went to study. Of those who migrated externally the regions to which they migrated were Barbados, Antigua, St Maarten, St Lucia, Florida, Jamaica, Trinidad, England, Canada, St Croix, Martinique and the US and British Virgin Islands. Clearly all had been temporary migrations and perceived as such by the women.

Personal History

The section of the survey questionnaire relating to personal history was deliberately placed later on in the interview in order to elicit more open and honest responses from the respondents. It was felt that by this time both interviewer and interviewee would have broken down the initial barriers which prevent freer communication between the interviewer and the participant in the survey.[2] The questions in this part of the survey attempted to collect very private data on the the respondents' reproductive, sexual and emotional lives.

Question 26 asked the respondents about the age of menstruation. The average age of menstruation was 12 years in Barbados, 13 in St Lucia and 11 in Dominica. Question 27 then inquired about the source of their information on reproduction and sex. The respondents in all three countries found out about sex and reproduction in fairly similar ways. The main difference among those surveyed was found by age group because written information had been more inaccessible to older women. In addition, older generations of mothers were less forthcoming on these matters which were considered taboo, and not openly discussed with young people. Some change had clearly taken place with the younger age group by which time the sources of information had increased to include the following: parents, mother, teachers, friends and books. Some learnt from more than one source, being introduced to some knowledge by a parent but finding out more from friends, or from books, or a teacher.

Question 28 asked respondents to say at what age they were sexually active. While some felt comfortable to answer this question, others were more reticent and there were also some "no responses" on this question. The no response rate on this varied between territories as well but was interestingly lowest in Barbados and St Lucia being only five in Barbados, and nine in St Lucia, compared to 20 in Dominica. At the time of the survey, three women from the sample in St Lucia and 11 women in Dominica said they were not sexually

---

[2]This was confirmed by our interviewers who had this experience in talking to the women. The women were at first reticent, but after the initial non-intrusive categories were covered, they were more prepared to speak about personal and intimate facts.

Table 5: Age of First Sexual Activity, Barbados, St Lucia and Dominica

	12	13	14	15	16	17	18	19	20	Over 20	Cannot remember	Not sexually active	No response	Total
Barbados	–	3	5	8	13	11	23	10	6	16	4	7	9	125
St Lucia	3	2	5	14	17	16	22	10	9	11	3	4	9	125
Dominica	1	3	11	11	18	9	14	5	13	8	1	11	20	125

active. The ages stated for first sexual activity ranged from 12 to 25. The following table gives a summary of age of first sexual activity by country.

More instructive than the stated age are the reasons given for becoming sexually active. This question is key to the subject which this study attempts to understand – how, where, why are decisions taken by Caribbean women and what are the determinants of these decisions. The question of first sexual activity is important to women as it also signals the possibility of childbearing. Thus it denotes for many women the shift to young womanhood or adulthood and, for some, an awakening of responsibility for their actions. It is useful to first illustrate why they become sexually active before a discussion on the issue. These reasons are listed along with the numbers who gave these responses.

Barbados: Felt ready (45)
Experimenting (24)
Peer pressure (7)
Old enough (5)
No reason, just happened (5)
Pressure from partner (3)
In love (2)
Teenager (1)
To maintain relationship (1)
Had the right partner (1)
Got married (1)
Seeing partner 2 years (1)
Not applicable (7)
No response (22)

St Lucia: Own decision (36)
Peer pressure (12)
Ready (9)
Curiosity (8)
Old enough (1)

Got married (4)
Pressure from friends and relatives (7)
Pressure from partner (6)
Pressure from home and parents, father (3)
Had found boyfriend (4)
Forced into it (3)
Pressure from partner and friends (2)
In love (2)
Ignorance (2)
Pressure from father to look for a man to support her (2)
Sexually abused by a family friend (1)
Did it because of home problems (3)
Not applicable (4)
Social pleasure (1)
No response (15)

Dominica: Own decision, own free will, ready (40)
Pressure from boyfriend (1)
Social pressures (16)
Peer pressure (10)
Curiosity (5)
Had boyfriend and/or felt mature (5)
Was in love (5)
Body pressures (2)
Don't know (2)
Rebelled against father (1)
Forced by father (1)
Steady intimate relationship (1)
Got married (1)
Ignorance (1)
Not applicable (11)
No response (23)

The responses to this question indicate the many ways in which women are introduced either gently, coerced by force, or through rebelling, to early sexual activity. There were significantly fairly easy responses to this question in Barbados, compared to the more enigmatic responses for Dominica. Peer pressure was clearly a very important reason in all three societies, but the large number who indicated that it was their own decision or that they felt ready suggests that they had given the matter some thought. Nonetheless, the wide range of responses which include pressure from partner, friends, or in some cases, forced by father, suggest that young women are unsure about the nature of sexual relations, may be misguided by traditional ideas of "keeping

Table 6:   Marital Status of Respondents in Sample

	Married	Common Law	Married* or Common Law	Visiting	Separated or Divorced	Occasional Partners	Partner Overseas	No Relationship	No Response	Total
Barbados	25	15	2	39	3	–	–	32	9	125
St Lucia	25	33	12	30	2	–	1	22	–	125
Dominica	20	23	1	40	–	2	1	38	–	125

*This category includes women who live with partners but their marital status is unclear.

a man" or may be powerless to challenge their elders. The distribution of responses, nonetheless, indicates that the majority of women appear to be in control of their sexual experiences.

Question 30 asked respondents about their present marital status. The largest number of women in all three societies were in visiting unions followed by those who stated that they were not in a relationship. The predominance of women in visiting unions followed by the two categories – married and common-law – also reflects a similarity with the past literature on union status in the Caribbean. In Barbados married women exceeded those in common-law unions (Table 6), in St Lucia and Dominica common-law unions were greater in number than married unions. In both Barbados and St Lucia several women stated that they were divorced or separated. When this overall pattern is compared to parent's marital status we find that the majority had stated that their parents were legally married. What may account for this disparity is the age of respondent's parents. Traditionally, as found in the WICP data, Caribbean women and men enter into marital unions after first being part of a visiting union, next a common-law union and then marriage comes at a later date. To support this argument, it was noted that most respondents had stated that their parents had children before marriage.

Questions 31 to 37 were questions which were ambiguously answered and differently treated by the various interviewers, thus it was not possible to adequately compare responses. These questions sought to elicit from respondents why they made the choices they did in respect of partners, whether to get married or live with someone, and whether it was their own choice to do so. In one case, a 31 year old woman who was born in Antigua, but was living in Barbados at the time of the interview, noted that she chose her first and second partners because she felt comfortable with them and was attracted to them. After a while she realized she had made the wrong choices because the first was very interested in having several relationships at one time and the second after a traumatic event in her life, decided that he would withdraw from her. She chose therefore not to marry either of them (062B).[3] A second case in St Lucia of a 41 year old woman is interesting as well. She is at present living with a common-law partner, whom she lives with for love reasons. Even though she stays in the relationship, she feels that her choice had not been the right one as she did not receive enough emotional and financial support from her partner, and she wanted to further herself but was not encouraged to do so. The choice to live with him was made because of the birth of her first child (042L).

The questions concerning number of children which respondents had (Table 7), age at which they had their first child (Table 8) and contraceptive use (Table 9) were fairly straightforward and yielded some informative data. Many of the respondents stated that they had no children, the largest number of those not having children being in Barbados (64), a fact not explained by the age distribution of the population which was fairly similar in all three societies (see Table 1). The only variable specific to Barbados which might explain this finding is that in Barbados we find the largest number of respondents pursuing and completing tertiary education. It was also pointed out previously that opportunities for employment, travel, and abortions or family planning advice were more accessible in Barbados. Of those who had children the majority had between one and three children, with only women in Dominica and St Lucia having three to seven children and one woman in each of the three societies having had eight children. Since this data on childbearing does not address completed fertility except in the case of 42 women out of the total number of 375, ie 11 percent of the sample, it is not possible to draw definitive conclusions about changes in family size. Nonetheless bearing in mind their experiences of parents' relationships, siblings, and other choices available to them, it is likely that there is a tendency for ongoing decreases in family size. The data support the notion commonly held that there is an inverse relationship between level of development and family size.

A variable proportion of women had their first child between the ages of 18 and 21. In St Lucia and Dominica 18 percent of the women had their first child between ages 14–17 compared to 9 percent in Barbados (Table 8). Of

Table 7:   Number of Children of Respondents in Sample

	0	1	2	3	4	5	6	7	8	No Response	Total
Barbados	64	30	19	4	1	1	1	–	1	4	125
St Lucia	35	28	23	17	14	2	3	2	1	–	125
Dominica	33	33	27	14	6	6	3	2	1	–	125

[3]Each of the 375 questionnaires was assigned a numerical code with the letters B, L and D to differentiate between the three societies. Where material is drawn from a specific questionnaire the code number is indicated in this way.

Table 8:   Age at which Respondent Had First Child

	14-17	18-21	22-25	26-29	30-34	Over 34	N/A No Children	No Response	Total
Barbados	11	20	11	9	5	1	64	4	125
St Lucia	23	44	14	7	2	–	35	–	125
Dominica	22	42	22	4	–	–	32	3	125

the women in the sample who had had children, the majority had their first child between 14 and 25 years of age. Of those who had children, very few had their first child over the age of thirty. If we compare this finding with the overall age distribution of the respondents (Table 1) we note that 222 women, or 60 percent of the sample, are under 30 years of age, and 148 were over 30, allowing for five no response on age. Thus there is still a significant number (132) who may still have their first child over thirty years of age. Different kinds of responses can be seen in relation to women and childbearing. A 32 year old respondent from Marigot in Dominica said that she has a good relationship with her partner who is sensitive to her needs, that she has already met her own goals in life, that of a professional career and maturity, but indicates no specific desire to have children within the relationship (008D). On the other hand a 39 year old senior welfare officer from Barbados has no children, was not in a relationship at the time of the interview, although she had done other things which she considers important in her life such as purchase her own home and furthered her education. She expresses a desire, however, to have children and start a family (019B).

Question 42 was felt by researchers to be a crucial one, indicating as it did a fundamental area in the lives of women – it pertained to the issue of who made decisions about contraceptive use and what method was used? This is best discussed after a comparative examination of the methods used in the three societies (Table 9).

The most frequently used method of contraception was the pill in all three societies, with the condom being the second most frequently used in St Lucia and Barbados. In Dominica, however, the injection was the second choice of women after the pill (Table 9). A startling figure was that of those who were sexually active a significant percentage stated that they were using no contraception, being 10 percent in Barbados, 18 percent in St Lucia and 20 percent in Dominica. Some of the reasons given for not using contraception were: "can't take pill because I'm hypertensive"; "stopped using injection because it made me fat"; "injection is not a good experience"; and "not effective – I got pregnant again".

Table 9:   Methods of Contraceptives Used

	Pill	Con- dom	Con- dom & pill	Injection	IUD	Rhythm	Tubal lig- ation	*Combi- nation and other	No contra- ceptives	Not sex- ually active	No response	Total
Barbados	28	18	6	–	6	6	1	13	13	13	21	125
St Lucia	25	15	3	4	1	4	2	8	23	7	33	125
Dominica	31	8	–	14	2	1	1	3	25	14	26	125

*IUD and Pill; Foam and Pill; Pill and Injection; IUD, Condom & Pill; Suppositories; Loop

Table 10:   Person Who Made Decision Regarding Type of Contraceptive Used

	Respondent	Respondent and her partner	Partner	Not sexually active	No response	Total
Barbados	39	30	3	13	40	125
St Lucia	33	33	4	7	48	125
Dominica	42	6	1	14	62	125

In Barbados and Dominica, 39 and 42 respondents, respectively, made their own decisions regarding use and type of contraception. Where the decision was taken by both respondent and partner, St Lucia shows the highest number of joint decision making, being 33, which compares favourably with Barbados (30). In Dominica only six women made this decision with their partners. Three women in Barbados, four in St Lucia and one in Dominica admitted that the partner had made the decision regarding contraceptive type used (Table 10). In the case of St Lucia the pattern of decision making over the sample was as follows: there was a high no response rate of 62 women, as noted above; 33 women said that it was a jointly made decision between themselves and their partners, 21 said it was an individual decision, four said that their partner had made the decision, and one indicated that it was made with advice from a doctor. Fourteen women stated that this question was not relevant in their cases as they were not using any contraceptives at the time.

The dynamics of decision making in regard to childbearing was a very nebulous area of inquiry. The responses between the three societies did not vary tremendously in this respect. Several scenarios occurred with frequency when the responses were pooled. Perhaps the most recurrent response was that the first child was unplanned, and that neither partner had made the decision. With respect to second and later children either both partners or the woman alone made the decision. In some cases subsequent childbirth was unplanned, or in a very few cases, the male partner made the decision. It appears that despite the tremendous services provided by family planning agencies, there is a gap between the delivery of these services and how they are received and absorbed by both women and men. In other words individual decision making is still contingent on personal choice, biological imperatives and "accidents will happen", hence the obvious difficulty of family planning services in responding to this complex issue.

The extent to which childbearing was a focal point of decision making in the lives of Caribbean women, or whether it was something which "happened" and around which they then negotiated their lives, must be considered here. In St Lucia, the question of childbearing was not applicable to 35 women in the survey who did not have children. Of the remainder, 42 said their children's births were accidents, while 28 said they had planned theirs. The rest of the sample had mixed responses on this question, with one woman stating she did not really know whether it was a planned decision in her life. Of the 11 remaining respondents, some of their children were accidents, while others were planned for, and not necessarily in that order of things.

Question 47 specifically asked whether the respondent would be willing to say if she had had any abortions and if so where was this done. It was expected that the response rate for this question would not be high, given the prevailing, largely moralistic, attitudes to the issue of abortion. It is useful to state the limitations on the data received for this question, bearing in mind that this data may be very distorted due to the delicacy and controversy surrounding the issue. Truthful responses with regard to abortion practices are difficult to obtain from interviewees. Question 47 asked "Would you have any problems telling me if you have had any abortions? If so would you be willing to say where this was done?" In Barbados 98 women said that they had never had an abortion, one person had a problem answering this question, 17 gave no response and nine admitted that they had had an abortion, all done in Barbados. Four of these were carried out in a doctor's office, four in a private clinic, and one in a public hospital. Question 48 followed this up by asking about whose decision it was to have the abortion, whether it was the woman's, her partner's, her parents' and so on. Six of the nine women made the decision entirely on their own, while for the remaining three, it was a decision taken jointly with their partner.

In St Lucia 108 women said they had had no abortions, four said they had, one stated that she had a problem saying yes or no, while 12 chose to give no response to the question. Of the four respondents who said they had had abortions, one woman indicated that it was carried out in Barbados, one at a doctor's office in St Lucia, while one did not wish to state where this was done. In St Lucia the decision to have an abortion was taken by the woman herself in one case, by the partner in another, and by the combined advice from partner and friends in the case of the other two women.

In Dominica, the issue was also a difficult one on which to elicit information, understandably so, from women. Ninety-two respondents said they had had no abortions, thirteen stated that they had had, one stated she had wanted to have one at the time of a pregnancy but could not afford it, one had had a miscarriage and 19 did not wish to respond to the question. Of the 13 who stated they had had abortions, 11 said it was done at the doctor's, one at a doctor's clinic and one abortion was done in Dominica. With regard to the decision to do so, 11 women in this country said they had made the decision themselves, while one said it had been a joint decision between herself and her partner. The other respondent did not answer this question. The issue of abortion remains a contentious, controversial and unresolved one in relation to family planning and reproduction.

Extracurricular Activities

The questions in this section were for the most part open ended, eliciting from the women who were interviewed a frank appraisal of their lives and of the decisions they had made thus far. This section of the interview which was designated "extracurricular activity" sought to expand the customary reading of the feminine domain, out of the traditional spheres of mothering, emotional relationships, and pragmatic concerns of making a living. It attempted to provide the women who were interviewed with the opportunity to examine their experiences consciously in order to assess decision making and choice in their lives, and to see if these choices were of their own making or were influenced by significant others around them. As was indicated by the field researchers and supported by the main researchers, this last section of the questionnaire allowed the respondents a moment for reflection and analysis of their lives, many intimating that they had never mulled over their cumulated life experiences, thinking them out chronologically and thus had never attempted to figure out why they had made the choices they did. Perhaps because it was linked to the idea of hopes and aspirations, and was also framed next to a conjectural inquiry which asked them to imagine the kind of life they would want to have if they were not limited for choices, the responses in this section provided us with some of the best insights into decision making in women's lives in the Caribbean.

Questions 54 and 55 asked the women if they had any special interests or hobbies outside of career and a family and whether they had been actively pursuing these interests. No response was received from six, two and four women in Barbados, St Lucia and Dominica, respectively. Thus the majority of women were willing to answer this question. The number who stated they had no extracurricular activities was 19 for Barbados, 50 for St Lucia and 38 for Dominica. Of those who stated that they had extracurricular activities and were pursuing these, we found the following picture of women's creative lives.

In Barbados, 14 women between the ages of 26 and 43 were involved in church groups. Eighteen were active in sports and here the age distribution was between 18 and 39 years old. Thirteen women between the ages of 16 to 39 were involved in service in professional and community organizations. Forty respondents from Barbados were pursuing a varied combination of activities including sports, welfare clubs, reading, craft, sewing, church and community service.

Of those who for some reason could not pursue extracurricular activities, we found four women who did not cite their interests but pointed out that due to lack of time, having to spend time in studying, career or family commitments, they were unable to pursue other interests. Eleven women, however, stated their interests and gave specific reasons why they could not pursue these. Among the activities they indicated an interest in were dancing, singing, water sports, going to the gym, church, service and community organizations and art and craftmaking. Some of the reasons they listed as preventing them from extracurricular participation were job commitments, studying, limitations of time, and in the case of water sports, the expense of doing so. An interesting feature of the responses was that the concentration of women's extracurricular activities in Barbados was in the traditional areas in which women usually find themselves occupied, such as in the service of the church and other community welfare organizations.

In St Lucia seven respondents between the ages of 17 and 32 years were involved in church activities only; six between the ages of 19 and 31 years in sports and 11 between the ages of 22 and 54 years participated in service or community clubs only. Thirty-four respondents had a varied combination of interests which they pursued. These included sports, church, community groups and service club activities, reading, craft, baking and dancing.

Of the respondents from St Lucia, 15 who did not engage in extracurricular activities stated their interests as well as reasons why they could not pursue them. The activities stated included sports, church activities, travelling, crocheting, reading and singing. Reasons for not being able to pursue these interests were limited time, having to take care of families, lack of motivation and losing interest. There were no explanations as to why 50 women in St Lucia stated that they had no extracurricular activities.

In Dominica the women who engaged in only one extracurricular activity were as follows: 24 women between the ages of 15 and 44 years were involved in church activities; six between the ages of 18 and 36 years pursued sports activities; five between the ages of 20 and 36 years were involved in community groups; and five between the ages of 35 and 42 years were members of women's groups, two of which had political affiliations. Thirty-one women had a combination of interests including sports, church, community, cultural and school organizations, dancing, reading and craftmaking.

Twelve respondents who did not have extracurricular activities stated their interests as well as the reasons for not pursuing them. The interests stated were women's groups, church and community groups, music, crocheting and sports. The majority of women stated that familial responsibilities did not allow them to explore their interests, some stated that time did not permit, while others expressed lack of motivation. One respondent stated her reason as resulting from her bitter frustration and depression. As in Barbados, the women in St Lucia and Dominica also tend to become involved in, or express interest in, activities which have traditionally been seen as compatible with femininity.

Of those who indicated that they had extracurricular interests, many were unable to pursue these interests. A 36 year old respondent in Dominica who had eight children between ages 20 to one and a half years old noted that she did not now pursue her hobbies of crochet and sports: "when I was younger I used to play cricket and netball, because I have children and time is scarce" (057D). On the other hand, a 37 year old woman in Barbados, who had one child when she was 20 years old and who works at present as a designer said that she actively pursues her interests of weight training, self defence and craftmaking (067B). The luxury to have and pursue extracurricular interests was contingent, by and large, on family size, time management of the woman, and whether some of the interests were compatible with religious and group affili- ations. Of the total sample in all three societies, 71 percent were able to engage in some activity related to their personal development in their leisure time.

Rating Major Decisions

Question 56 asked the respondent to consider what in her opinion were the most important decisions she had made in her life. This question proved to be a difficult one for some of the women as the idea of ranking the decisions in their lives had never occurred to some, or more accurately perhaps, they did not perceive decision making as a conscious process. In this respect there were no responses, or a response of "not sure, don't know, no major decisions, don't think I made any so far," from 17 women of the sample in Barbados, 26 in St Lucia and 23 in Dominica. The remaining respondents indicated several areas in which they felt they had made major decisions and these can be grouped under the following categories: Children, Career, Education, Religion, Self Improvement, Relationships, Sexuality, and Abortions (Table 11).

Question 57 followed through on the issue of decision making and asked women how they would rate the major decisions they took in their lives in terms of importance. For those who listed a series of decisions, it is useful to look closely at the way in which they rank their choices. In Barbados, 71 respondents stated two or more major decisions, and some had made up to five major decisions. The remainder of the sample cited one or none. In St Lucia, the number who cited more than one decision was 55 and in Dominica it was 54. In an attempt to see what was the decision most cited, we are using

Table 11:   The Most Important Decisions Women Have Made in their Lives

	Barbados	St Lucia	Dominica
Decisions related to children including: Not to get pregnant, not to have children, not to have children early in their lives.	36	26	20
Decisions related to career.	19	18	18
Decisions related to education.	36	11	37
Decisions related to religion and moral self development including: becoming a Christian, giving Christ my life, to be a good woman.	14	8	9
Decisions related to self improvement and independence, including: to migrate, to move away from family, to buy own house.	13	19	15
Decision regarding relationships including: making own choices, raising children in nuclear family, to get married, to stay in or to move out of a relationship.	14	25	14
Decisions regarding their sexuality including deferring sex, abstaining from sex, moving out of an incestuous relationship, abstaining from sex and remaining chaste until married.	5	2	3
Decisions to have or not have abortions.	5	4	1

*Totals are greater or less than 125 because in some cases respondents stated more than one important decision, and in other cases could not locate anything as an important decision.

those who listed more than one choice and those who cited one only. For those women who did not give a response to this question of ordering decisions, some had difficulty in saying what were the major areas of decision making and in some cases they stated that it was too personal to indicate what these were. The final figures tallied here, and as indicated in the related Table 11, exceed 125 as some women could not rank decisions on the basis of one or the other category, but tended to group them as equally important in their lives. Despite this obfuscation of a clearly convoluted area of life, as we group those categories which do emerge, they point to women's perceptions of the major areas of decision making in their lives. It is also useful in this examination to locate the differences, if any, between one society and the others.

It must be noted here that these designated categories are by no means discrete, and are very much related to the continuum of individuals' lives. It is very difficult in the question of decision making to determine a ranking. We must, instead, see decisions which women take as being influenced by the experiences of their youth, whether they had early access to education, training, jobs, contraceptive information, parental guidance and so on. In seeking to understand the dynamics of decision making in the lives of women, we are more and more convinced that the decisions which women articulate that they make, are in many cases "made for them" by the circumstances they find themselves in. In retrospect age and experience allow them to understand that these were turning points in their lives. For example, Joan from Barbados was 40 years old at the time of the interview. She is one of four children born to her mother, a nurse, and her father, who had worked as a postman. Joan fulfilled her early career goal of becoming a teacher once she completed a Bachelor's degree in Education and a Teacher's Certificate in Education. However, with marriage and a new baby she opted to change jobs, but remained in the field of education as an Education Welfare Officer. This job was a more flexible one in terms of time and thus allowed the time she needed to spend with her two children. The decision to have two children, she cites as one of the major decisions which she has made in her life. The other major decision which she states as important is becoming an independent working woman. Joan plans to pursue post-graduate studies, but for now, her children remain the obstacle to her realizing this goal since she feels that she needs to spend as much time as possible with her children until they are old enough to manage on their own (024B). Norma Jean from St Lucia is 38 years old. She could not complete her secondary level education because she needed a job to maintain a child, so she dropped out of school and became a kitchen helper at an hotel. She was ambitious and while there were limited jobs to choose from, she later on became a telephone operator and receptionist at the same hotel. She continued to have children, having three more and entered a common-law relationship with the father of her last child as she felt that her children needed to have a father. Her last child was born to the partner in this supportive common-law relationship. The major decisions that Norma Jean cites in her life are her decision to purchase the land on which her house is now situated, and the decision to build a house of her own. At present she is continuing her education as she feels that lack of education has been a major obstacle, limiting her choices in life (067L). Catherine was born in Dominica to a single mother and was one of six children. At the time of the interview she was 40 years old. She had eleven years of primary level schooling and proceeded on to her first job as a substitute primary school teacher. Her second and more permanent job was that of Village Council Clerk which she took because it paid more. The major decisions which she has made in her life are having her six children, having them live with her, and her choice of partner who she describes as responsible, hardworking and reliable. Despite the joys of motherhood, having the children and her limited level of education are the major obstacles which limit her life choices (056D).

Returning to the rating of most important decisions, we discuss the various responses elicited under the headings which follow.

Children

The first major area of decision making was in relation to children: either to have or to not have by means of abortion, to defer sex until marriage so that they would not have a child, "not to get pregnant at an early age", to defer sex until they were personally ready to deal with the responsibility of children, and to return to their society or leave a marriage or long standing relationship for the sake of their children and family. The number of women for whom decisions related to children ranked as the major one they had made in their lives was 36 in Barbados, 26 in St Lucia and 20 in Dominica.

Career

A second major area of decision making was that of pursuing a career (in addition to marriage and childbearing in many cases). The numbers here were very similar for all three societies, being 19 in Barbados, 18 for St Lucia and 18 for Dominica. This again reflects the consciousness of women that the jobs they are now choosing are actually careers, as for instance women working in agriculture or non-professional jobs, or those who create jobs for themselves. In several cases the women said the major decision in their lives had been to leave one job or career and seek another which gave them more satisfaction, in some cases it being a job of their own creation, as in returning to farming, craftmaking, sewing/dressmaking and opening their independent businesses.

Education

Under the category of decision making demarcated as education, there was a marked difference between the younger and older respondents. The younger women who would have had greater opportunity for education more readily identified education as one of the major decisions in their lives thus far. What is also at issue here, is that they have had to make fewer choices in their lives by this time, and thus would identify the area which most preoccupies them at present – education and a career. In Barbados 36 respondents indicated that either pursuing education at tertiary level, or completing primary and secondary level education was one of the most important decisions made in their lives. Surprisingly the response rate was very small for St Lucia, with only 11 women stating education as one major area of decision making. For Dominica, there was a relatively high rate, with 37 women identifying education, especially continuing education beyond primary level as being a major area of choice. This is a significant finding with regard to decision making and aspiration. First there is clearly a similar process occurring in Barbados and Dominica with regard to definitions of gender identity – education and career are interlocked with the notion of independence in a struggle for another definition of womanhood/femininity which is becoming delinked from marriage and childbearing. In Barbados, the existence of a university campus certainly allows greater choice for women. In other words, it appears that while traditional ideas of the society, that womanhood is only proven by bearing a child or children, still hold fast in the Caribbean, there is a simultaneous process at work. Women are consciously breaking down these stereotypes by adding new criteria to this definition of their femininity, one which involves education and/or a satisfying career.

Religion

Another major area of decision making emerged and the findings are worthy of investigation, possibly calling for more in depth scrutiny in future studies of this kind. The first is women's association with religion, and Christianity in particular, since this is the dominant religion cited by the respondents. Fourteen women in Barbados, eight in St Lucia and nine in Dominica included the following kinds of responses with regard to religion: "to become a good Christian"; "to give Christ my life"; "to live for Christ"; "to get closer to God"; "to live a Christian life"; to find a place to worship; to be baptized; build a spiritual foundation and a sensible relationship with God. Studies on women's relationship to religion are very necessary because their attitudes to religion inform many other choices they may make in their lives as for example to have abortions or not, the kind of woman they see themselves as in the society, the kind of relationship they want to have with their families and their partners, and so on. Religion still provides a fundamental guide for masculine and feminine roles in society. The extent to which women remain religious also prescribes the range of choices they are likely to make, or the roles they feel they are required to perform.

Self-improvement

The fifth major area observed from the data was the *acknowledgement of their own needs for self-improvement*. This covered a range of activities which included their desire for full independence, to take control of their spending, to take charge of their own lives, to take responsibility for their children's economic needs, to buy a house on their own, to move from their parents' home to live on their own, to move out of a relationship with or without the children to live on their own, the desire to further their education, or the need to migrate. In Barbados 13 women cited their search for self-improvement as the major area of decision making in their lives, in St Lucia 19 chose this area, while the figure was 15 for Dominica.

Relationships

An area of decision making which one would expect women to cite as major in their lives is that of sexual relationships, whether that of making their own choice, getting married or staying in a common-law relationship, keeping the relationship together because of children, or leaving it because they feel the need to be independent from a partner. In Barbados, 14 women cited decisions in this area as the primary ones. Interesting and significant as well is the figure for St Lucia which is 25, while the figure of 14 for Dominica is comparable to that of Barbados. The responses of the questionnaire invariably set up the notion here again that the choices were made independently by women, with little evidence of consultation with, or lack of support, from partners, parents, siblings and so on. The responses in this area were also integrally linked with the needs of children, so that it is difficult to separate the choices women make in this area from those responses which were related to children cited previously. The dominant finding of this study is that a large proportion of children are born before stable unions, out of legal unions and that common-law marriages still prevail among the majority of working class women. Decisions regarding relationships, therefore, tend to be closely linked to the presence and needs of children, the quality of support from a partner and, in some cases, the social and economic benefits to the woman if she shifts from one kind of relationship to another type. There was a difference in the case of Barbados where the sample chosen had a predominance of professional, educated women and urban women. The difference in Barbados may also correspond to historical associations with the notions of respectability related to class, colour and race in this society, which were more definitive than the other two societies. More women in Barbados appear concerned about the social acceptability of their union status.

Sexuality

The last area is that of sexuality. This relates to a very small number of the sample, but it is crucial to discuss the responses under this category. In Barbados, five women indicated that to not have sex, to not have sex at an early age, to not have sex and get pregnant and ruin their lives, and whether or not to have sex before marriage were major decisions in their lives. In St Lucia two women cited factors associated with an understanding of their sexuality, one indicating that it was a decision to leave her job as a result of sexual harassment. In Dominica, three women cited this as an area of major choices in their lives, with two decisions being given as moving out of an incestuous relationship and abstaining from sex to remain chaste until marriage. While few women ranked this as a major area of decision making, when the responses for the categories of children or relationships and contraception are tallied with this one, we can conclude that the area of female sexuality, and choices which women are making with respect to the separation between their sexual pleasure and reproduction, appear to be very informed ones.

Abortion

Under decisions to have abortions, four women in Barbados stated that they had rated the decisions to not have abortions and keep the babies as major choices in their lives, with one stating that having an abortion was a major decision. Four made a similar choice in St Lucia with one woman stating that it involved *keeping a second baby and feeling good about it.* In Dominica one woman indicated that a major decision in her life was to bear five children and not to abort them. The responses to the questions both on abortion and whether or not women include this as an area of decision making remain hazy. The subject itself is either dealt with openly by the woman if she has no qualms about it, or closely guarded by others who feel uneasy about it. In fact it would appear that women are more open about whether they have chosen to not have abortions rather than when they do so. Those who stated this as an important area of decision making, demonstrate that it is clearly an area in which women deliberate when they become pregnant. It appears to us that the decision to not abort indicates to the woman herself that the "occupation" of motherhood has been a very conscious choice among other choices.

Obstacles to Achieving Goals

Question 58 asked the women who were interviewed to state what they thought were the major obstacles in their lives limiting the things they had wanted to do. Two major differences between the responses gleaned from the three islands could be seen at a glance (Table 12). The first variance is due to the difference in the overall age structure of the sample in Barbados as compared to those of St Lucia and Dominica, with the sample in Barbados having had a higher level of educational attainment than the other two. The second is due to the different opportunities for education and advancement available within the societies themselves, with Barbados having greater opportunities for education and careers, St Lucia having some scope and Dominica clearly offering the least possibilities for recognized advancement in professional careers within the society itself. The range of obstacles cited were grouped under eight broad categories. Each of these categories will be discussed in some detail with comparisons made for the three societies. Under this question some women cited two or three responses so that the total number of responses exceed the numbers of the sample. More than one half of the sample in each society listed two or three obstacles, with the majority stating three, the most regularly cited being "money, education and children".

By far the most serious obstacle cited as limiting the aspirations women have for their lives was that of lack of finance or money. While some women simply stated lack of finances or money as the obstacle here, others qualified this by stating that finances were lacking either to further their education, to

Table 12:   Major Obstacles to Achieving Goals

	Barbados	St Lucia	Dominica
1. **Having Children** being pregnant; being single parent; postponing education until children are grown.	18	39	38
2. **Education** not completing; not being attentive in class; not having wide range of skills.	12	39	57
3. **Unemployment** not having job; not enough opportunities in areas of interest.	11	10	14
4. **Family Responsibilities** over protective parents; pressure from father; lack of care from mother.	7	10	11
5. **Money** not enough finance to further education to pursue course of interest.	61	52	67
6. **Time**	4	1	–
7. **Self-development** not being self-confident and assertive; people trying to put you down; laziness; chronic indecision; indiscipline re time; procrastination; being in Caribbean (3rd World) with limited opportunities; being ill (epilepsy); visually impaired; being too involved with friends; society; boys.	18	7	8
8. **Partner** husband did not approve of one working; separation from husband; fear of marriage; husbands' extramarital affairs; getting married early.	2	7	6
9. **None**	7	5	5
TOTAL	140	170	206

*Totals are greater than 125 because in some cases respondents stated more than one obstacle to achieving their goals.

fund their own businesses, or to build houses of their own. In Barbados, 61 women cited lack of finance as an obstacle, 52 women in St Lucia cited money and 67 in Dominica cited money.

The second obstacle preventing women from achieving their goals in life was that stated as children. Having stated children as the response though, many women qualified this by saying the children were not to be blamed, but if they had had support to look after the children, or if they had themselves deferred childbearing, had not got pregnant at an early age, were not single parents, they could have got on with their ambitions. Some of them were simply waiting for the children to grow up sufficiently to begin pursuing their own interests. There was very little rancour in the matter of fact way in which women expressed "children" as an obstacle to their own development. Again in Barbados, due to the younger ages of the sample, only 18 women cited children as a problem, in St Lucia 39 cited children, while in Dominica 38 gave this obstacle.

The third hindrance to their aspirations was that of lack of education, although here some of the women blamed themselves for lack of attentiveness and for not completing their primary schooling. To a greater extent they linked the problem of further education to lack of finances to continue education or to having children to support and care for, which in turn prevented them from accessing further education. Education, however, is clearly seen as a major avenue through which women feel they can satisfy their aspirations, with finance being viewed as the means through which they could achieve higher education or more skills for employment or possibly higher status in society. As discussed above, due to the actual sample difference there was wider variation in this figure, with 57 women in Dominica stating education as an obstacle, 37 in St Lucia and 12 in Barbados.

The fourth obstacle was that of unemployment or lack of work. While this was a relatively small group it is useful to pull out the numbers who actually stated unemployment as the problem. This figure was four women in each of the three societies. Following closely as a problem area was that cited as lack of opportunities in the home society, and again in this respect there was a significant and crucial difference noted between Dominica, St Lucia and Barbados. Eleven women in Barbados and 10 in St Lucia stated that there were not enough opportunities or areas of interest to pursue a career or the vocation they wanted, while 14 women had this problem in Dominica.

A fifth area was that of their own agency or self-perception, referring to their lack of self-confidence or assertiveness, lack of discipline, poor time management, laziness, illnesses of one kind or another, or becoming involved with boys and partying. Some feel they have been prevented by friends or society from doing freely what they wanted. Eighteen women cited these kinds of problems in Barbados, but again because of the age structure, this suggests that these problems were due to youth and inexperience of life. In St Lucia seven women cited these kinds of problems, while in Dominica eight gave reasons such as these for not making decisions or getting what they wanted out of life thus far. Under this category some reasons were cited in terms of the attractions of migration as offering them a better life. For instance those residing in Dominica stated that being in that society was an obstacle, others stated that not being in the United States or not having a visa for the United States was a problem.

The sixth major area was that cited as family responsibility or problems associated with family. This included problems such as the overprotectiveness of parents, grandparents who disallowed personal decision making, pressure from one father, and indifference from mother. Seven women cited these as obstacles to their control over decision making in Barbados, 10 in St Lucia and 11 in Dominica.

The seventh area was that of marital problems of one sort or another, as for instance separation from a husband, husband's infidelities, an abusive partner, fear of marriage, getting married too early in life and rushed into an early marriage. While only two women cited these reasons in Barbados, where because of the age structure of the sample this is perhaps expected, in St Lucia this statistic was seven and in Dominica it was six.

Finally, it is heartening to note that in each of the societies several women stated that they had had no obstacles in their lives thus far preventing them from making decisions or achieving goals. The numbers who stated no obstacles were seven for Barbados, five for St Lucia and five for Dominica.

Aspirations and Desires

The final question of the interview schedule, question 59, asked women: "If you were not limited by anything, money, place of residence, education and so on, what kind of life would you like to have as a woman?".

Women's relegation to the private sphere of life in general has created the prototype of a female personality which is largely pragmatic, and the notion that their lives must be centered around the "impulse to mothering" [Senior 1991]. This is an implicit message which is transmitted by many women to their girl children. This same relegation to household and family has also demarcated the acceptable goals to which women are likely to aspire within any society at any given point. Question 59 was appropriate at the end of the study on aspirations and dynamics of decision making. The survey had taken the women through a review of their lives, and the actual decisions they had had to make thus far, into a personal evaluation of the limits of their present achievements, and a critical self-examination of where they would like to go in the future. The final question allowed the respondents the imaginary freedom to envisage the kind of life they would ideally have liked to have if they were not restricted by the limits of their own life experiences. A summary of the major responses is displayed in Table 13.

There were marginal differences in the responses of the three societies, but there was also a marked similarity in the regularity and groupings of responses which all women gave to this question. We analyse first, the regularity of responses by type in all three societies. Some women gave several responses

Table 13:   The Kind of Life Women Would Like to Have

	Barbados	St Lucia	Dominica
Career			
Own business or career, *including*: being career woman, getting job and supporting self, supporting family, becoming a nurse, doctor, flight attendant, and hotel manager.	47	44	56
Religion			
Religious life *including*: perfect Christian life, do charity work, do work of God, help less fortunate, especially less fortunate women, community activities, respect and respectability.	29	28	27
independence			
Independent life *including*: making own choices, being a free woman, making all my decisions, free, single and independent, good standard of living, respect with a position in society, independent working woman.	24	27	25
Children			
To have (1, 2, 4) children *including*: would not marry but would have 3 children, get married and have 10 children, adopt family, single life with children, live quiet life with partner and daughter, two children, a boy and a girl.	32	30	20
Travel			
Travel abroad to pursue career, as tourist, for education or for a carefree life.	14	8	12
Education			
To go back to school to become educated, to go to university, to educate children, to develop a wide variety of skills.	14	7	7
Wealth			
Including: Luxurious lifestyle, higher level of income, acquisition of a house, car, money and land, being a happy woman, living and eating well.	13	13	5
Involvement in Politics			
Including: political activism for women and human rights, helping women,			

Table 13:   The Kind of Life Women Would Like to Have (Cont'd)

	Barbados	St Lucia	Dominica
Involvement in Politics (cont'd)			
helping the elderly, helping other people achieve something, working with groups involved in charity, remedial education.	9	10	4
Satisfied With Life			
Living the kind of life I want right now, lives one day at a time, does not want for anything, the ideal does not exist.	7	2	4
Not Sure and No Response	7	10	9

* Totals are greater than 125 as respondents stated more than one aspiration as important.

which straddled different areas of life. As such the total responses here again exceed the number of respondents per country. The responses which occurred most frequently, nonetheless, indicate the greatest aspirations which these women have in life.

The responses labelled "career woman, getting job to support myself and family, or identifying the kind of career they want to pursue" as well as indicating the importance of having their own business or career as women, were by far the most recurrent ones; 56 women in Dominica cited these as what they would like in life, 47 in Barbados, and 44 in St Lucia. To a large extent the first category of responses, that of career, could hardly be separated from another major grouping, that of children which included marriage, family and number of children a woman wanted in Table 13. There were a few women, however, who stated unequivocally that they would be very happy to be married, stay at home, be a housewife and bring up their children if it were possible. Thirty-two women in Barbados indicated this as the goal that would make them happy, 30 in St Lucia and 20 in Dominica.

Respect and dignity and being good to others figured very highly in women's aspirations for life. This was rated as the second aspiration which women cited and was linked, not surprisingly, to religion and to having a decent and respectable life, involvement in charitable activity, leading a "perfect Christian life, pleasing to God, and helping the less fortunate". Twenty-nine women in Barbados cited this area as important, 28 in St Lucia and 27 in Dominica. Service to community was closely followed by a third set of aspirations – that related to "Involvement in Politics" which dealt with women's desire to help other women, to struggle for equality for women, to work for human rights, to help the elderly, the infirm, or young people. Those who wanted to become politically involved were nine women in Barbados, ten in St Lucia and four in Dominica. If these two sets of statistics are cumulated, then the number of women who cite areas outside of their own personal well being, is 38 in Barbados, 37 in St Lucia and 31 in Dominica.

Having said this, however, there was also a group of women to whom full independence, living a single life or having control of their economic life and personal freedom were very important goals. While some of these women were equally concerned with the needs of others, they, nonetheless, identified individual freedom and independence as a major aspiration in their lives; 27 women in St Lucia could be grouped in this latter category, 25 in Dominica and 24 in Barbados.

Travel and luxury competed evenly with education as aspirations which women had, with travel taking the lead in these three. Fourteen women in Barbados said that they would like to travel abroad, one indicating that she would like to be a rich professional tourist. Twelve women in Dominica said they would like to travel overseas, some to pursue their career, some to have a carefree life, some to temporarily enjoy a carefree life. Eight women in St Lucia said they wanted to travel widely, one qualifying that she would like resources to travel worldwide.

Wealth was important to women, but not unduly so given the small number who viewed money as the crucial ingredient for happiness. Financial solvency was in general linked to having a well paying job which allowed them to support their family and relatives, which gave them independence from a partner, or a sense of satisfaction about being a woman who was not dependent on anyone for a livelihood. There were a few, however, who openly declared that luxury was important to a happy life, they wanted money so that they would not have to work, one wanted a "fat bank account", another wanted money so that she could have land, home and a car, another wanted money so that she could centre her life around her children, while one woman in Barbados stated that she wanted to be "the richest woman in the world". The number for St Lucia and Barbados here was similar, being 13 women in each of these societies, while five women in Dominica focused on luxury as the key ingredient to giving them the kind of life they wanted.

Education was a key area in women's lives. The desire for education can be linked to development of a career. Many women wanted careers which were dependent on further education. Those who specifically cited that "they wanted to go back to school, to go to university, to educate their children, to get as much education as possible or to develop a wide variety of skills" were 14 in Barbados, seven in St Lucia and seven in Dominica. If we tally these figures with those indicating business and careers as important then the number of women valuing careers determined by having skills and education is as follows: 63 for Dominica, 51 for St Lucia and 61 for Barbados. If additionally we add to these two categories the number of women who identified independence gained with education and careers or own businesses, then the responses for these three aspirations combined are 88 for Dominica, 85 for Barbados, and 78 for St Lucia. We need to recall here that the same women gave several categories of responses to this question, so that this statistic measures the regularity of responses rather than the actual number of women. In total, therefore, 68 percent of the responses in Barbados, 62 percent in St Lucia and 70 percent from Dominica linked women's aspirations to education, career and independence. What emerges from this exercise is that education, own careers and independence figured as the most important aspirations of the majority of women in the sample, and key factors in fulfilling their perception of an ideal life.

Two other categories must be noted with interest. The first is that of a no response to this question, being 10 for St Lucia, 9 for Dominica and 7 for Barbados. Some of these no responses were "don't know" or in the case of two women, "do not believe that the ideal exists" and "I live one day at a time, the ideal does not exist".

There were also responses which were gratifyingly optimistic about the quality of women's lives in the Caribbean. Seven women in Barbados, four in Dominica and two in St Lucia gave the following kinds of responses to this question of life's ambitions: living that kind of life now and waiting to build my dream home, already living it, satisfied with my life, have everything and not want for anything.

Marked Differences and Similarities in Aspirations Between Women of Barbados, St Lucia and Dominica

One major area of dissimilarity in the responses needs further amplification. This was the attitude to marriage. The number of women stating that marriage itself was an important factor, and marriage with children was key to their happiness was greater for Dominica and Barbados, than for St Lucia. In St Lucia for instance several women gave the following kinds of responses: "living on my own and in control of my own life", "independent with a visiting relationship", and "free and single", "single with my own children". In Dominica and Barbados while there were many advocations about independence, there were also responses which reiterated traditional notions of an ideal nuclear family situation, such as: "happily married woman at home", "married life", and in the case of two women in Barbados to be married, "have a family", "employed", "pursue further studies and be happy", and "two children (boy and girl), continuing happy marriage and good health". In the case of one woman in Dominica the response was "happily married woman at home"; "not as a housewife but home manager". The notion of mixing both career and family may not represent the aspirations of the total population of women in the three societies, but it certainly emerges as a major ongoing dilemma which the contemporary economic situation presents for women, given the fact that motherhood and career have become more incompatible as occupations shift from home and farm related, to public and private enterprises. The distinctions between different priorities which women admit to as individuals, the goals which they set themselves, and the pragmatic decisions they have had to make in their lives are not transparent ones. The relationship between aspirations and actual decisions continues to be a very elusive one to pin down, continuously unfolding in unanticipated ways, yet possessing an internal logic that becomes apparent only in the long term. The final chapter of this study (Chapter Seven) brings all of the major findings of the study in dialogue with the main question we set out to answer – what are the dynamics of decision making in the lives of Caribbean women from Barbados, St Lucia and Dominica?

Selected Life Histories of Women From Barbados, St Lucia and Dominica

In this chapter we select a number of life histories from the larger sample of taped interviews carried out with women in the three societies. They represent an integral source of data against which the responses elicited from the questionnaires are examined. Of the 23 life histories collected, scripts of three women from Barbados and St Lucia and four from Dominica are transcribed here. They were selected to represent the different age groupings, levels of experience, including completed fertility, and levels of education found among the various women interviewed. Pseudonyms have been given to the women to ensure confidentiality.

Barbados

Glenda

Glenda was born in Barbados in 1963. At the time of the interview she was 31 years old. Her mother is a self-employed cosmetologist, ceramist and flower arranger and her father is a retired journalist. Her parents are legally married and have a fairly stable marriage which produced three children – Glenda and her two brothers. Glenda attended preparatory school, Queen's College, a secondary school in Barbados, and the University of the West Indies at Cave Hill, Barbados, where she completed a bachelor's degree in Public Administration, and teacher's college where she completed a diploma. She is married with two sons and has spent only one year outside of Barbados, when she lived in Canada.

Glenda considers the decision to get married as being significant in her life. Her alternatives were pursuing postgraduate studies or choosing a career path which would have taken all her energies, leaving little time for anyone else in her life. While she cannot point to the actual reason why she chose marriage, she thinks that her parents' stable marriage which has lasted for 35 years and the fact that she had known her husband for a long time, may have influenced her decision to get married. She does not regret the decision she made.

She feels that a marriage is incomplete without children. While not having children does not mean the end of a marriage, to her it is worth much less without a child "to shower love upon". Having children has made her marriage stronger and given her and her husband "something in common because [before] we didn't have anything in common". She had problems with conceiving, so that her first child was planned through a process of fertility control, four years after she got married. Assuming that she would be unable to conceive without fertility control, her second child was conceived accidentally.

Glenda's choice of career between accounting and teaching was largely influenced by her plans for a family life which included children. Inflexible and long working hours for both parents would mean that children would always have to be left with someone. She was, therefore, sure that her career choice could not compete with her partner who was already working as an engineer with long and inconsistent working hours. She therefore chose a career in teaching which would give her flexibility and time to spend with her children, unlike accounting which would sometimes have required long hours at work.

Her mother and two brothers had migrated to the United States and she had been left to take care of her father. She feels that this responsibility may have fallen to her because she is female and she feels that this was unfair to her as she should have been allowed to make the decision for herself. This situation meant that she and her husband lived in her parents' house. They moved from her father's house to in-laws after a quarrel between her husband and father in which she decided to take the side of her husband. While the episode caused her some pain she did not think twice about moving out with her husband. Her view on life is that with age and maturity, attachments shift from mother and father to one's husband and children.

The choice to live in Canada was made when she decided that she wanted to pursue studies in geography. Not being able to manage the fees despite doing odd jobs, Glenda had to discontinue; but, on returning to Barbados she taught geography. Her reason for having chosen to study and teach this subject is that she "could do it well". She went on to explain that "a lot of things I do and I can't explain to you why".

Glenda's education for her career was interrupted by her choice to postpone postgraduate studies while she bore and raised her children. She still feels that she needs to defer studies until the children have reached an age where they are comfortable and can cope with their studies. She is more resolute about postponing studies since she feels that her children are not coping as well as they ought to because she is unable to spend more time with them. The children's time, when she feels that she ought to be with them, is spent watching television, playing and reading books. Her feelings of guilt result largely from being female, in that, it is easier for her husband to be more detached from the children because children have higher expectations of a mother's closeness and involvement in their lives, than they expect of fathers. Having children also influenced her perception of herself. According to Glenda, "you don't realize how mortal you are till you have children. You are always praying that nothing happens to you. You get a mortality check the day you give birth."

Glenda remains committed to education but feels that she will leave general teaching to focus on researching specific areas within education. Her experience with her own children who seem to perform better with male teachers has given her the idea to look at problems such as how boys relate to classes compared to girls, why boys are not achieving, curriculum development and new strategies for teaching. Her hopes for her children are to see them grow up and attend university, and for her husband, to keep him happy.

Bernadette

Bernadette is forty years old and was born in Barbados. Her mother was a housewife. She died when Bernadette was five years old. Bernadette lived with her father, who worked as a security guard, and her sister until age thirteen when her sister moved out. At this point she became totally responsible for managing the household. Bernadette became a teacher after receiving training in a teacher's college. Teaching had never been her first choice but she had to postpone her hopes of pursuing a career in law due to financial constraints. Despite this she still maintains her dream of one day becoming a lawyer.

At age 23 years Benadette was faced with a major decision of whether or not to get married. The decision was a particularly difficult one since marriage would have meant relocating to Canada and she was committed to raising her nephew whose mother was in Canada employed as a nurse. She made the decision that leaving would have disrupted too many lives and thus did not get married at that point in her life. When she finally did decide to get married she had by then attained a Master's degree in Learning Disabilities and Reading, had travelled widely and was very active in church and community activities. In retrospect (during the interview) she realized that part of her decision not to get marrried at age 23 was not only the responsibilities she felt she had to members of her family but also that she herself had not yet achieved many of the goals which she had set for herself. At that time marriage would have limited her ability to pursue these goals. ". . . there would be the urge to do things that I would not be able to do . . . now there is not this urge . . . I am settled".

Bernadette is married with one child and lives in Christ Church, Barbados. Her child, though welcome, was unplanned and she has made a decision that she will not be having more children in the near future. This has largely to do with the fact that she has recently changed jobs and feels she needs some time to get used to her new job before having another child. Whilst she does not view career advancement as ultimately more important than children, she feels that career development and stability will provide the environment and stimulation which would be best for children. In fact with a career she would be able to spend less time with children but feels that her experience and development would allow her to make that time "quality time", while being at the same time financially able to provide the best for the child or children. She feels strongly that she could not raise her son on her own since as male he identifies strongly with the males around him (father and grandfather). As a female she would never be able to fulfil these role models.

Having a son has made Bernadette very sensitive to the realities of males in Barbadian society. As a teacher she has experienced the ways in which boys are "punished" if they are seen to be achieving, especially in areas which are considered female. She is happy to see though, that despite these pressures on young men, especially in a society like Barbados which she describes as "not very demonstrative" more and more men are becoming active in childrearing. Bernadette sees the relationship between mothers and their sons as significantly contributing to the irresponsibility of the male which continues to be a main feature of the society despite a perceptible increase in their participation in family life. The reaction of many men to an upward movement of women, in terms of their education and career, has been one of resentment which, in her view, has resulted in an increase in domestic violence. While she in no way condones violence against women, she fears that the advancement of women and the aggressiveness which seems to go with this independence, is having a negative effect on men in particular and the society in general.

Mary

Mary is 43 years of age. She was born to common-law parents and has seven sisters and three brothers. She also had an 'outside' sister who was born to her father in the same year that Mary herself was born. Her mother had helped her father to build the home in which they lived and "when he started giving trouble she left him and built another house for herself". The break up of the family resulted in Mary spending some of her young years with her aunt. She attended elementary school only, got pregnant and had two children. She then worked for three years at a garment factory. She left the garment factory when she again became pregnant in 1975 and spent the years until 1993 having and taking care of four more children. Mary is not legally married and lives with her partner who is the father of her four youngest children. She has never lived outside of Barbados.

A very important decision which Mary made in her life was to "get up and work". Her children were getting older and their father spent a lot of his money drinking. While he provided some income to take care of the children, he did not provide any for her needs so she had to find a job in order to support herself.

During the relationship which produced her first two children, she was living with her aunt who was angry, but supportive, for the first pregnancy. With the second, however, her aunt decided that Mary should discontinue seeing her partner. He, unlike her, had continued through secondary school during her pregnancies. All Mary's children were unplanned and she states that she did not want to have so many children. It was difficult to plan her pregnancies because she cannot use the pill because of a problem with varicose veins.

Mary had to spend her childbearing years without working for an income because there was no one else to look after her children. Conditions at home during this period were "not too bad". She got money for groceries and clothes for the children though they didn't have as much as some other children. She, however, "didn't have all that she needed". By the time she decided to begin working again in 1993, all her children were old enough to take care of themselves and she could therefore spend some of her earnings on herself.

Mary is dissatisfied with her living conditions at her partner's aunt's house where they are living at present. In addition, her relationship with the children's father is one where they hardly speak to each other, but her economic situation means that she has to continue living with him to be assured of a home to live in. She thinks it is important to own a home, for the independence it will give her, but sees her chances of saving enough money to acquire this home as almost impossible. She plays the lotto regularly with the hope that one day she will win enough to support herself and her children.

She has now entered a more rewarding outside relationship but would not be willing to live with the man since he also lives with his family. She, however, would consider marrying him if he asked her though she is not totally sure that she wants to get married because "marriage don't really last". Marriage is therefore something which she would not actively pursue but rather "if it happen, it happen".

Mary's life experiences have informed her attitude to raising her children. She thinks the decision to stay home with them always making sure that they were comfortable was a good and important one. This also provided a base from which they could all achieve secondary education, which she has never had and had to pay the price for throughout her life.

St Lucia

Virginia

Virginia was born in St Lucia and is now 27 years of age. Her parents, now separated, used to live together in a common-law union. Her mother is a retired teacher who runs a pre-school and her father, a retired police inspector, works with the courts. She has three brothers and a sister from her parents' union and "a lot of half brothers and sisters, some born before and some after they were living together". Virginia, at the time of the interview, was enrolled in the first year of the Bachelor of Arts in English and Linguistics at the University of the West Indies. Through the distance teaching programme she was able to pursue her first year in St Lucia while she continued to work as a teacher. She is a single woman, has no children and lives with her mother. She taught after leaving secondary school and took a two year break to pursue a Diploma in Teacher Education at the community college.

Virginia considers one of the major decisions in her life is delaying childbearing until she has completed her education despite the fact that she "badly" wants to have children. She therefore makes sure to use contraceptives. She feels that someone without a university degree has no guarantees for securing a job and, in addition, she feels that an advanced education will enhance her own personal development.

She loves children and feels that they are necessary to continue her lineage. Though they will provide some security for her old age, she sees them primarily as providing comfort and pleasure. "Children are so funny. You get so much humour; they're fun to be with and I think I want to experience that with my own and I think I have a big contribution to make because I think I know how to raise children". Virginia's experience at raising children came from helping her mother to raise her nephew from the age of four years when his mother moved to St Croix. She also spends much time with her godchildren.

Children do not necessarily mean marriage for Virginia. She remains very cautious especially because of her experience of living with brothers and a father who always had many women at the same time. She feels that, on the whole, St Lucian men are not genuine or honest and are noted for having many women, a situation which she cannot tolerate. If married to someone she would not want to let the person go, but neither would she put up with him seeing someone else. Virginia also feels that marriage may inhibit her to the extent that the commitment to someone else means that she would always have to take the other person into consideration, making adjustments and compromises which she does not feel she is ready to do right now. Her aim in life, at this point, is to be a fairly complete woman; one who is equal to any man.

This means being confident about myself, attaining a particular level of education and being able to do different things. I am a trained teacher but I want to also be more than that. If you're only competent at one thing and something happens, you have nothing to fall back on. A lot of men get a number of skills and can move from job to job. My one big wish in life is to publish my writings. I write poetry and short stories and I think I want to publish a novel – I want to become a writer.

Her decision to become a teacher was partly a pragmatic one and partly fulfilling one of her goals. While growing up she was interested in writing, law and teaching. On completing Advanced level examinations at 17 years old she had no money to pursue a law degree, nor a career as a writer, so she sent out applications and accepted the first response which was a teaching position. She rejected subsequent responses which may have been more lucrative because she had already made a commitment to the teaching position which she had accepted. She will stay in teaching for a few more years because this job allows her time for herself on evenings, weekends and during school holidays when she can write.

While a male figure may be of some importance in raising a child, Virginia feels that this is not necessary, especially when the relationship is not a healthy one. She has seen many single mothers raise children who grow to be healthy children, and married couples where the men have very little to do with their children except to reprimand them now and then. Because of this, and the fact that she wants to prove to herself that she can be a good parent without the help of a male, she would like to be a single parent for at least the first of the three children which she wants to have.

Due to her experience of her brothers as "womanizers", her partners are never chosen from the community in which she lives. This is so partly because she fears that their acts may result in men (perhaps brothers of the women whom her brothers have been with and treated badly) causing her hurt; she fears that the local men may want to avenge their sisters' ill-treatment at the hands of her brothers. Because of her view that women cannot expect to change men once they get into a relationship with them, and her dissatisfaction with the attitudes and behaviour of the young men in her community, Virginia is extremely cautious about entering into a relationship with any of them. She admits though that at about age 30 years she thinks men appear to settle down and they begin to be more responsible towards their children, though she is not sure how much more they are responsible in the home generally. Her experience with her brothers doing housework only when their mother is away makes her feel that perhaps if given a chance, men would do more.

Continuing to live with her mother and brothers (her sister moved out when she got married) is a decision which Virginia is comfortable with. She makes a financial contribution to the running of the home and has adequate privacy and independence.

Martine

Martine was born in St Lucia in 1957 and at the time of the interview was 38 years old. She is the ninth child of twelve siblings, eight girls and four boys. Her father is now dead and her mother is 73 years old. Her father was engaged in a number of different jobs, being at one time a carpenter, at another a fisherman and later in life a tailor. Her mother was self-employed, selling products in the market place. Her upbringing was a very traditional one, the girls were treated differently, were overprotected and taught to carry out household tasks. Her brothers had much more freedom. All of them, however, had the freedom of the family land which was large "like an estate" and in which they pooled labour and time together like an extended family.

She first had a primary level education, but in the early days there was little access to secondary education for girls from working class backgrounds in St Lucia. There were not many schools around and she failed the entrance exams to St Joseph's Convent, the best secondary school for girls. She was sent on to vocational school to do secretarial training, home management and also basic subjects like English. She states that at present there are more than twenty-two secondary schools in St Lucia.

She did not complete her vocational education although she began acquiring various certificates of competence. A teaching vacancy arose when she was 17 at a primary school and she took up employment instead. She did not have a choice in the matter of completing her vocational education. Her sister was funding her through vocational school and after some time argued that her salary could finance her own education rather than that of Martine's. While teaching, however, Martine continued her education, doing the annual teacher's examination, a secretarial course, a certificate course in Youth and Community Development under the Commonwealth Programme and a University of Guyana Diploma programme. She has never migrated to live out of St Lucia, but she has travelled to other Caribbean countries and to Israel for short term courses.

A major decision she has made in her life is to go to Guyana to pursue the diploma, leaving her daughter who was only ten months old at the time. She herself has had three children and she says that she regrets having them to some extent because they have hindered her personal development. This experience has led me to have a different attitude towards raising my own daughter.

Not because you are married you have to have children, and you must think about the effect that children have on your life. I learnt about the need for a woman to be financially independent in St Lucia after I had my first child. Even though I was in a legal marriage the man was flinging around with different women, was very insecure because I was more educated than him, he therefore saw me as a threat.

Another major decision she has made is to not get married again despite continued proposals from her present partner. This decision was based on her experience of her first and only marriage. In the present relationship she earns more than her partner and although he is very supportive she "fears that somewhere down the line he may do something displeasing to me and I may have to have a separation. Because of that I am playing it safe."

Her main aspiration is to be self-employed and in charge of her life. This would increase the control she has of her present life, and her ability to cater to her children's needs and to allocate time for her relationship.

Her general comment on women's attitudes to men is frequently encountered among Caribbbean women like Martine who have some measure of control over their lives. She remarked in the interview "women feel that if they don't have a man then they are missing out on life . . . one of the positive things I gained from my parents was the value of working for what I want to achieve. I am doing the same for my children now."

Juliette

Juliette's mother, who was a housekeeper at a hotel and is now a pensioner, and her father, who was a contractor and builder and is now dead, lived together in a common-law union. She has one sister who is a teacher living in New York and two brothers, one works at the lighthouse and the other is a supervisor in the government service. Juliette, like her mother, works as a housekeeper at a hotel. Her education stopped at the primary level because she was unsuccessful in meeting the grade to go on to the secondary level. The education system at that time was different from the present system in St Lucia where success at the common entrance guarantees a place in one type of secondary school. Other types of secondary schooling now exist for those who are not successful. In addition her mother's attitude was different to that of mothers nowadays. Her mother did not encourage her the way she (Juliette) now encourages her children and makes sure that they get a proper education. Had she had the opportunity to continue her education "I would be able to do better now". She would have been able to realize her ambition of becoming a nurse, she said.

Juliette's first job was at 15 years old when she worked as a trainee waitress in a hotel. The hotel in which she started closed down and she relocated to another where she spent the next 15 years, with some breaks for childbearing. During the period of raising and caring for her child she was responsible for the housework. "I was like a slave, I never had time, because he didn't want to help me in the home". Juliette's husband was seeing other women and had two or three 'outside' with them. She believes that he treated her unfairly as she was dependent on him as breadwinner. In situations like these women can make use of the Women's Desk's programmes when they are experiencing these kinds of difficulties. These programmes are provided either by government or non-government organizations such as church organizations. Juliette explained that "when you are going through problems with men and you go to the Crisis Centre, you go there because you haven't got nowhere to run and you have no finance for a lawyer. You are going through the problems and you can't take anymore. But, she says, they are not helpful enough. If you could afford a lawyer you would".

She then went on to give her own experience of going to the Crisis Centre where they promised to write her husband a letter. Her husband's response was that he was not going to see them. She was subsequently sent to a lawyer whose cost would have been $5000.00. Of course, she was in the same position she had been in originally when she visited the Crisis Centre because she could not afford to pay the lawyer, therefore could not employ his services.

Juliette is now divorced and has three children, one girl and two boys. She had her first child when she was 23 years old. She did not use family planning methods because she had heard many women complain about side effects. "Some claim that when they take it they get pregnant so I never bother – it is not safe." On the basis of this both she and her partner had agreed not to use contraceptives.

The unfair treatment she received from her husband resulted in Juliette leaving him after 15 years to go back to live with her mother. She then began working as a laundry attendant in a hotel. Having left the children with their father, she would go every afternoon to cook for them and make sure they were well and cared for. The decision to leave the children was largely to ensure that her ex-husband was forced into a position where he would have to maintain them. He did for about two or three months then he left them without saying anything to her. She has since been both mother and father to her children.

Dominica

Pamela

Pamela was thirty-eight years of age at the time of this interview. Born in Dominica, her primary schooling was done in Castle Bruce, Dominica, but she has also attained tertiary education in a community college in Virginia, USA, where she first did an associate degree in education and later a bachelor's in liberal arts at a university in the same city.

Her mother was a farmer and her father a retired police officer. Her parents were not married and she was the second of her mother's three children, the other siblings being a brother and a sister from her maternal parent. Her father had other children in his marriage. She has on the paternal side two sisters and five brothers. After her birth, her mother also got married. She recalls in her own upbringing no difference in the treatment between her brother and sister. Her brother was taught to do housework just like the girls and can still use the sewing machine "just like us".

After primary level education in Dominica, at the age of fifteen, she taught in a primary school for thirteen years. At the age of 28 she went to community college and university in Virginia. After this she came back to Dominica and from 1989 began working with an organization involved in developing small agricultural projects, SPAT. Until 1990 she remained with this organization as a women's programme officer. She contested the general election in 1990 for the Dominica Labour Party. She lost the election but thought that the experience was a good one. It was the first time that a woman had contested the constituency she did, and she was able to relate political issues to women's issues. She met people at varying levels of the community and thus developed a greater understanding of people's lives in Dominica. She returned to work with SPAT in the same year.

She was married but is now divorced. She was married two years after arriving in Virginia to a Dominican man who had wanted her to come to visit him in Virginia but did not entertain ideas about her going to school while she was there. She decided that her role was not that of supporting him while he was in college, but began a process of furthering her own education, starting with education in a teacher's college, an area in which she had had a lifelong interest. While developing her degree in teacher's education she switched to the component which focused on women's studies, impelled by the idea of herself as a self-driven and ambitious person.

Her decision to leave the marriage was one of the most important ones she has made in her life. The first major decision was to go to Virginia, the second, to begin studying. She had actually been living with her husband in Dominica for fourteen years and had never thought of marrying him. She thinks that the environment of the USA coupled with the alienation of being away from Dominica led her to seal the relationship with a legal contract of marriage. The legal ties also assisted in getting her daughter to Virginia with her. Her daughter had been living with Pamela's mother but she wanted to bring the family together in one place. It had been a very difficult decision to make to leave her daughter at age six with her mother and go to Virginia, but her mother encouraged this move, and was very willing to take over the care of her child.

The divorce resulted from an increased amount of tension in the relation-ship after she and her husband returned from Virginia. While there he had initially been supportive, she says, but he came back from Virginia very "macho", and actively campaigned against her, especially during her bid to enter politics. The tensions built up to an overwhelming pitch during her political lobby, where he misbehaved publicly, causing destruction to prop-erty. When she tried to get help for him, realizing that his actions were those of a psychologically disturbed person, he threatened to kill her. His abuse was largely emotional rather than physical but this affected her daughter's mental health and led her to make a decision about the divorce. Having made this move, she approached a lawyer and carried through with the proceedings, including the change back to her maiden name, to cut all ties. By this time there was no resistance from her ex-husband. She claimed no child maintenance nor alimony settlement, she just wanted to be out of the difficult situation of her marriage.

Carla

Carla was born in Dominica in 1951 of mixed parentage. Her mother was of Carib, Indian and African descent and her father was English and French. Her mother was a housewife during Carla's childhood but now runs a guest house. Her father was an agricultural extension officer and is now deceased.

Carla had many years of primary and secondary education, going to preschool in Roseau, primary school in two different villages and subsequently to the Convent High School for girls in Roseau. She did not, however, obtain her GCEs and left school after her father died to help take care of her siblings, of whom she was the eldest of ten children.

Her own personal life was, as for many Caribbean women, a chequered one. She got married when she was very young. As a follower of Roman Catholicism she took her vows very seriously, but separated from her husband after twenty-one years of marriage. It was a very hard decision to make, one which she still has not resolved mentally. She took the children when she left the marriage. They were 18 and 20 years at the time, and being young adults by that time, they helped her to leave. Carla had stayed in the marriage that long because of the children, and left as soon as she felt they were old enough to handle the breakdown of the marriage. She now has another five year old boy but does not know who the father is.

Her working life was a full one, and continued throughout her married life. The first job which she held for several years was in the accounts department of the Caribbean Development Corporation. After this she worked in Roseau exporting fruits and vegetables. Finally she started her own business called Sun Trading where she sold tyres, motorcycles and related goods.

She left the island of Dominica to visit her children in the USA and spent a year with them. When she returned to her husband she closed down the business and also left him. She then began to run a restaurant but leased this out after two years. At present she works with a tour company.

The major decisions Carla asserts she has made in her life are to separate from her marriage after twenty-one years, and to go into her own business. The area of her life in which she has never actively made a decision is in that of childbearing – none of them was planned, they "just came".

Marigold

Marigold is 42 years old, born in 1953 in Dominica. Her parents were labourers, her father was married with 14 children and her mother was single, with seven children. She finished primary level schooling and would have liked to continue her education: "Well today I would not be where I am. I am sure I would be living a more independent and comfortable life." She left primary school and began work at an estate picking up coconuts to maintain herself and to help support the younger siblings. She continued to work in agriculture moving on to the banana industry where she worked as a banana washer. She believes that there are more opportunities in other Caribbean territories such as St Maarten where jobs are more available and they are better paid. However, she thinks greater advancement is possible out of the Caribbean, as for instance "the USA. This is the land of opportunities once you have ambition". She herself has never travelled out of Dominica.

By age nineteen she began an active full-time relationship and sexual life. At age 21 she had her first child. She now has five children, ages 21, 19, 18, 16 and 7 each of whom is by a different father. Two of the children's fathers are overseas, three live in Dominica and the last one is her present partner. She and her partners welcomed the birth of the children although in retrospect she thinks they came too soon after each other. But she says, "It is good to have offspring to benefit from your works."

Outside of work and family, her special interests are going to a political women's group. But she is unable to rate the decisions or to state what were the most important decisions she made in her life. "I wonder, all that has happened to me I have not decided. They just happened." The major obstacles in her life limiting the things she wanted to do were having children, lack of money and the level of education she attained. If she were not limited by anything, what she would like to have is "a comfortable Christian life, running my own business".

Sheila

Sheila is 17 years old and lives in the Carib territory with her grandparents who are both farmers. They adopted her when she was nine months old. She attended primary school for seven years and went on to secondary school where she completed the studies but was unable to sit the CXC examinations because her grandparents did not have enough money to pay for the exams. She left school in 1994 and began working as a volunteer with the Sineku Adult Education Programme where she continues to provide her services. She also gives voluntary service to the Dominica Planned Parenthood Federation on an ongoing basis. She worked for two months in a temporary position with the Ministry of Agriculture. Sheila's experience of giving voluntary service and working in community development is typical of many women in Dominica, who use this avenue, when that of formal education fails, to achieve occupational mobility. She receives no financial benefits now but feels that her volunteer activities will give her the necessary skills and experience which she will need to be successful later in life.

Sheila, at the time of the interview, was awaiting responses from job applications which she had just sent out. She also hopes to further her education especially in the area of nursing which she wants to do as a career.

Official and Unofficial Interviews

This chapter includes summaries and relevant points of interest which have emerged from interviews carried out with a variety of resource persons in each of the territories surveyed. These interviews provide a background against which the questionnaire data and life histories are tested for points of analytical clarification. The resource persons interviewed were all involved in working with women, and specifically in the problems associated with family planning services in each of the islands. The long association and experience of these respondents with regard to women's choices have provided them with insights which are vital to this study.

Mr Charles Pilgrim, Executive Director, Barbados Family Planning Association

Family planning services in Barbados are relatively highly developed, with 90 agencies operating throughout the country. Clients develop alliances with nursing staff through counselling and interaction and retain good relations with the staff of the clinics. In addition to the pill, intrauterine devices and spermicides are available in shops and drug stores. Perhaps due to this ease of availability, there has been a decrease in client flow to the clinics, but a consistent purchasing of contraceptive aids, as some clients buy for others as a means of cutting down on bus fares.

The termination of pregnancy was made legal in Barbados in the Medical Termination of Pregnancy Act 1983-4 making abortions legal in this country on almost any grounds including financial ones. Paragraph 4 of the Act states that:

1) The treatment for the termination of a pregnancy of not more than 12 weeks duration may be administered by a medical practitioner if he [or

she] is of the opinion, formed in good faith (a) that the continuance of the pregnancy would involve risk to the life of the pregnant woman or grave injury to her physical or mental health; or (b) that there is substantial risk that if the child were born, it would suffer such physical or mental abnormalities as to be seriously handicapped

2) The written statement of a pregnant woman stating that she reasonably believes that her pregnancy was caused by an act of rape or incest is sufficient to constitute the element of grave injury to mental health required by subsection (1)(a).

This measure sought to deal with the old system by which some women had access to abortion through the medical system, while the less privileged women used backstreet abortionists. Despite the introduction of this act, there is under-reporting by practitioners. A tax is imposed by the government for abortions so that legal reporting means payment of the tax to the government. The freedom to have abortions legally has also brought its own problems. Some issues pertaining to termination of pregnancy and contraceptive use in Barbados were openly discussed in the 1986 address by Miss Billie Miller through the Ministry of Health in Barbados.

The availability of abortion and the widespread access to contraceptives have not resolved some of the pressing issues which affect women and men in relation to planning families. Among the most serious of problems were the use of abortions as a contraceptive method, and the persistence of teenage pregnancies despite the availability of contraception and advice on family planning.[1] Factors such as the above have led a pro-life group of Barbados to write a letter to the state in 1994 to request a repeal of the Medical Termination of Pregnancy Act.

Mr Pilgrim cited many reasons for shifting trends in this society, a society which has a well-developed infrastructure, a high literacy rate, and allows compulsory education to all until age sixteen. This coincides with the age of consent which is also sixteen.

He noted that the Chief Magistrate, a woman of humble beginnings who improved her status through education, had announced that she wanted a child but had no intention of getting married. This trend among professional educated women clearly influenced other women in the society. He commented on the lack of achievement among males suggesting that the education system privileged girls. Teachers were inclined to favour girls who became more academically successful, while boys pursued other interests such as

---

[1]Statistics at the Queen Elizabeth Hospital between 1982 and 1983 show that there has been a total number of 8,401 abortions registered for teenagers for this period, but a decline in the actual percentage per annum from 33.3 percent in 1982 to 20.5 percent in 1993. The total number of teenage births has also shown a decline from 4,450 in 1982 to 3,390 in 1993, or a percentage decline from 23.4 percent to 21.2 percent.

football. He also commented on the increasing unemployment among men and employment for women leading to an escalation in domestic violence, and the attitudes of some women who adhered to the notion that "a woman expects a man to beat her to tell her that he love her". According to his view women needed to shoulder responsibility not only for getting pregnant, but for further emasculating the Caribbean/Barbadian male. These problems he noted were higher among the black population of Barbados as compared to the white or other smaller ethnic groups.

Ms Roseanne Richards and Mrs Joan Cuffie, Interviewers for IPPF Questionnaire in Barbados

These interviewers were questioned on the administration of the questionnaire, the limitations of the questionnaire itself in approximating the 'truth' in the answers given by respondents, and some of their own perceptions of various issues with which the study concerned itself in relation to women of Barbados. They are both residents of Barbados; Ms Richards is a Barbadian, Mrs Cuffie a Trinidadian.

They both noted that no provision was made for guardianship in Question 40, on the assumption that this was not a legitimate category to be included. The responses on Question 47 have to be treated cautiously since in answering whether they have had abortions, women are generally guarded on this matter. There were also not enough questions asking people why they had not had children. While the questionnaire was, admittedly, a long one, it nonetheless enabled women to think about their lives consciously in relation to their partner and to assess their own needs.

Barbados' culture revolves around the idea of "people knowing your business", and the need to keep personal things close to your chest. Barbadian women have a tradition of 'hustling' as for instance in individual schemes for the preparation of food, but they are not amenable to jobs such as that of domestic helper. There is therefore a great difficulty in getting domestic helpers in this island.

There is a perception in Barbados now of the existence of more male single parent households with men adopting a nurturing role and taking care of their children. There are also more progressive acts of legislation passed in Barbados in relation to women's special needs, such as the family law acts.

Barbados appeared, to those from the islands of St Lucia and Dominica, as more developed, with people from those societies coming to Barbados to look for jobs and educational opportunities. They feel, however, that St Lucians are "treated badly" in Barbados, although they have a reputation of being "very bright". Barbadians perceive the two islands of St Lucia and Dominica to be fairly similar.

Mr John La Force, Director, Planned Parenthood Federation, St Lucia

Officially, the Family Planning Association was founded in August 1967. The initiative behind the establishment of family planning services was due to an observation by field workers in the social services that there were significant numbers of people who had large families, almost six or seven children per woman. At the time of its establishment, there was a heavy political involvement in the formation of the Family Planning Association as well as a tremendous reaction to the services being offered. A lot of people, as late as 1977, were accusing the FPA of trying to lead young girls astray and encouraging them to spoil their lives, of killing children, of putting chemicals into their bodies. In St Lucia there is at present a fairly large middle class and small working class. The people of the lower classes are less literate so although there are now 51 health centres, with no person in rural or urban St Lucia being less than three miles from a centre, full use is still not made of the services.

One of the reasons behind this was the importance of childbearing to women.

There was some myth, maybe out of religion, that if a woman does not have a child, she is cursed in some way, so every woman must try to have their womb blessed by having a child. A woman is not complete without a child. I know many women who do not have a child, they deferred child bearing because of a career. And other women would chastise them and say you're cursed, you can't even have a child. There were even names for women who could not have children, like barren or blocked tubes, or a patois term which I can't recall now.

Mr La Force's observation over the years is that there is now a stagnation in contraceptive use in St Lucia. This can be accounted for because of the following problems:

a) Communication in St Lucia where a lot of people are bilingual, but a lot of people are rooted in the creole, so that they cannot understand information conveyed to them in English.

b) Lack of knowledge of biology and understanding of how their body works. A lot of people do not understand the working of the pill, they don't take it regularly, and for instance women take the pill with a cup of tea for breakfast and go to work in the field and they see the effects of this in later years.

c) Use of *obeah* or *garde* consulted along with medical advice. The *garde* is the man who can see into the future and there is a great reliance on his advice.

Changing Attitudes

People will no longer say that they don't like the pill, but that they see the benefits of it – they can relate to the fact that whereas their mothers had eight children, they must do something at any cost to improve their lives.

The rates of pregnancy are decreasing in St Lucia but they are still high. As more women than men are completing tertiary education and choosing careers, contraception has become one more conscious choice they are making in their lives. This has improved particularly since the 1970s, noticeably especially in the Roseau valley area, when opportunities, including increased schooling were made available to more women. Nonetheless, the majority of women start to think seriously about contraception only after the birth of their first child, usually by age 20. Among those who are tied to rural agricultural situations there are many problems still. There is still poor attendance of children at school because parents rely on them to help with the harvesting of bananas and other crops. The farm situation is conducive to early sexual intercourse, to incest and rape: "he come onto me and then I get pregnant" is the cry of many women.

Abortions have always been accessible to women with means in St Lucia but are still illegal. There have been other legal changes which have attempted to deal with the relations between men and women in this society. There is a high percentage of men who do not support their offspring, but in 1994 the Social Welfare Act was amended to ensure that programmes for child maintenance were treated more seriously.

I think part of this problem has to do not so much with contraceptives but with attitudes to sex. I have seen in the past women fighting over men – there is an imbalance in the sex ratio here, but not at some age groups – so this does not account fully for the competitiveness among women.

Women have now learnt more control through education. They travel, they educated themselves, they recognize that they can no longer depend on men. 90 percent of the graduates from the Sir Arthur Lewis Community College, where tertiary education is available in this society, are women. They are now dominant in the public sector and visible in the legal services. Women who choose not to be mothers now are those who have a heavy professional schedule – there are a few of those in St Lucia and among these many are going on to do their PhDs.

Men stick together in groups now, they push drugs, or listen to music or play dominoes. If women sit doing nothing they will feel useless – women are more industrious. Some women work in the fields early and still come back to feed their men. What accounts for the difference in attitude to work between men and women? I can't put it down to slavery because this does not explain what happened in the 1950s and 1960s when greater migration made jobs available to men, so men were employed. I think now it has to do with lack of employment but more so lack of apprenticeship schemes of some kind within the education system. Women are trained and made responsible through the home – where do young men get that training? There is nobody to keep the young men in check now and this is crucial in a population where almost 50 percent are under the age of 20.

While the family planning services clearly direct some of their attention to male contraceptives, of the two methods, vasectomy and the condom, only the latter receives any attention. Men dismiss the former as "interfering with their electricity supply". On the whole, men are highly suspicious of women, although this is not transferred to the offspring. They recognize and are proud of their offspring, a man likes to be the father of a son. When we appeal to men through education not about the sex act but the consequences of child-bearing to the lives of their children, they are more attentive. Their antagonism to women is based on the idea that women always want something, particularly money, out of them. Interestingly enough, while they are willing to take responsibility for their offspring, this is not offered to the women who bear these offspring. The idea is that women are adults and are responsible for their own actions.

There have been different attitudes emerging among men though. First the fear of AIDS, second the social welfare people cracked down on them for support, and thirdly, women themselves demand greater attention. Today's woman is about ten times more intelligent than the men. A very young man said to me that his girlfriend is so bright, "I can't understand what she is saying, I have to go back to school to talk to her."

Aspirations and Decision Making Regarding Migration

In the 1950s and 1960s more men migrated, but the channels for migration are different now, and they are more open for women who want to migrate for educational purposes. Having said that it is still not easy for young women to migrate as it is difficult for a single young woman of 18 for example to get a visa for the USA, as the authorities fear she will go and get married and stay. On the other hand there is migration to the other Caribbean islands and to Venezuela and Latin America rather than to the traditional French ones of Martinique and Guadeloupe. Women view migration as a way out, but not in the same way that men do, men seek labour contracts, women seek to be educated, to better themselves.

Most women would want to do their education and come back, but in the process they get married. A lot of women who did not have children before might go, but some might have left a child or children and so come back. Women always have some connection to bring them back. Also, they feel they are not within the mainstream of the metropolitan society. The younger women tend to migrate I think when they feel the society is too small for them.

Gender Relations and Aspirations

A growing number of women are having children between ages 30-34.

I feel that women think they are incomplete without a child, so that they just have a child with any man, and to hell with the man – Every woman I have spoken to wants a child with or without marriage. I don't know of many men who get married and do not have children, although a lot of them have children and do not get married. I wish I could have an answer for why women want children.

The idea of modernity for women is that they do not want to get bogged down. For instance, some of the girls who have unplanned pregnancies go to Barbados and have an abortion. Modernity does not present a challenge for men:

I don't know what is wrong with men – fewer and fewer men go to tertiary education, more pushing drugs, doing nothing, I see the same trend in St Lucia in the rest of the Caribbean. The women on the other hand take more initiative. There are jobs available for men, like farming, driving, and so on, but the men feel that they should be in jobs which pay better wages, while the women create a lot of jobs for themselves, such as sidewalk hustling. Women just go and start a business and it works, I don't know what it is about men.

Women aspire to wanting to be highly qualified, to be independent, to work, to earn their own money, to have just the kind of things which men want, a nice car, nice house, but all women I think want to have a family. Her urge for independence is to make sure that no man controls her, and she gets the man in the process anyway.

Mr La Force's Recommendations

We need to change teenage behaviour before the teenagers enter childbearing years. How much information does a teenager really have before reaching this period? We need to bombard them with structured information on contraception, family planning, life, education and so on.

A greater focus on young people in the education system, as well as targeting those who work in agriculture can encourage changes in behaviour with regard to sexual activity, contraceptive use, and engender more harmonious relations between men and women in this society. There is a growing respect among men for women in this society, but the predominance of female teachers, the insufficient space for repeat students and the power of the education staff to decide who should or should not drop out of school, lead to high failure rates and lack of opportunities for those – particularly male students – who are trying to improve their condition.

Dr Seurage, President, Planned Parenthood Federation, St Lucia

Family planning services are not only interested in delivery of contraceptive devices, but they are trying to match the resources of the country with the fertility, and certainly with greater population growth than resources, one cannot expect improvement in the quality of life. I would say that the family planning services have made an impact on the society. About 15 years ago you would see many pregnant women, especially young women, on the streets. This is no longer the trend, both in Barbados where I worked before, and in St Lucia.

One of the problems I feel is that the schools are getting more aggressive and at secondary level more boys are dropping out, they are becoming a big problem in St Lucia. Male sexuality is about satisfying ego, the Caribbean male is still coping with the problem. The solution cannot rest solely with the education system in that culture in a society is transmitted through other agents as well – for example the 'garde' is still a dominant part of this culture. And very backward ideas are held on to – for instance the idea that a cure for venereal disease is to sleep with a virgin. The main thing one can notice from programmes which are geared for re-education is that you may stay in town and think you have the answer to the problem, but when you touch base in a little rumshop and chat with the group, you realize that you have not even touched the surface.

A little boy growing up . . . all he deals with is sex and women. Saying things on TV and Radio pacifies us at the Planned Parenthood Federation, but they have not touched the public yet.

Mr Willie Fevrier, Director, Dominica Family Planning Association

The Family Planning Association in Dominica was started in 1976 and was incorporated in 1981. Before this service was started, the government had provided family planning services to the population, but the new institution was geared primarily towards providing information and education about the planning of families.

Dominica is dominantly a Catholic society so that family planning services were viewed in a very negative light. Despite this disapproval, women have always been at the forefront of the promotion of family planning and of course they are the major users of the service. At the beginning they needed to use the services secretly but there is greater openness and acceptability now, although there are still problems for young people who fear to be seen openly using the clinics provided in the communities. The range of services available is now much wider in Dominica, including education and advice at the clinics, outlets where condoms are sold, or health centres which dispense a range of contraceptives at no cost. In addition, in the private sector, the pharmacies sell contraceptives without prescriptions, and there are private doctors and health centres which also provide contraceptives.

There are, however, still negative attitudes about the effects of contraception on the body,

For example a lot of women fear using the coil as there is a rumour that the child will be born with a coil in its hand. Or for instance, with the injectable contraceptives, if women do not see the flow of menstrual blood every month, they fear that this is accumulating every month and that it is unhealthy for the body. I don't know if I really understand this concern of women. Perhaps it is due to the fact that a lot of people do not read instructions or information handed out. This is why in this country counselling is key for the majority of clients. Unfortunately, nurses do not have the kind of time needed to deal with each individual client.

With the AIDS scare, more men are beginning to take responsibility for their sexual activity; more men are coming to the clinic for condoms, but by and large, it is women who still take on the major responsibility.

Decrease in Family Size

There has been a decrease in the size of families even in my lifetime.

As a boy I would identify several families with 8, 9 or 10 children, something which would not be so common today. There was a certain kind of pride in having a lot of children for both men and women. For men there was a pressure to start a family but my impression is that there was not the same priority for a woman to establish her ability to have children. It was important for a man to show that he was a man by fathering a child. For instance if one of my friends in his 20s had a child it was a big occasion for him and he would ask the other fellows around him when they were going to do the same. Of course there are other ways in which manhood was defined among us, for instance having several women, and if we don't have children with all, at least having a child with one woman. But the real decline in family size now is due first to the lower mortality rate for children – in the earlier days there was a separate section in the cemetery for children and this no longer exists, and second, due to the cost of bringing up a child now and the expectations which parents have for children – to feed and clothe them properly, to educate them. I think this is a conscious thought of both men and women.

What Are the Things Women Focus on?
Is Childbearing Central?

Childbearing is important for a woman. Education as an aspiration is not always fully satisfying. Many women have children when they are not ready, and most have at least one child. I think they may make a conscious decision that they want at least one child and when they want to have it but this does not always work out.

Perhaps women want to have children because of their more caring nature. I think men are caring as well but women seem to be more so than men. For instance, even among teenagers many of them at the time they are pregnant do not want the child but from the time the child is born they cherish the young one. More and more we see men doing this as well — you can see pride, ownership and love for these infants.

More women are deferring childbearing to find a job or career because with a job they can then earn and purchase what they want, including independence. Independence on this island for either men and women is difficult as jobs are not easy to come by. There is a high rate of migration to the neighbouring islands of Antigua, Montserrat and other islands around. For instance a woman would migrate to Antigua and do domestic work which she will not do in Dominica. A lot of migration also takes place to Guadeloupe and Martinique, mainly to the north of the island and very rarely to the south to Barbados for instance. I don't think that women and men in Dominica migrate because the society is not "metropolitan" enough for them. It is primarily a means of making money so that they can send home for parents and children. Some of them go to get an education as well and combine work and education. Their aspirations are not simply to leave Dominica.

Another area to which Dominicans go is St Thomas which is becoming more and more attractive than Martinique and Guadeloupe as the US dollar can be found there. Thus between the decline in fertility and the loss due to outmigration, the population in Dominica is itself decreasing. There has been a distinct shift regarding migration in the aspirations of women now as compared to two decades ago. More women now want to go abroad to get an education. Two decades ago they would have migrated primarily for economic reasons. When they are educated some of them return, but most of them stay abroad because they cannot find a suitable job here.

Male/Female Relationships in Dominica

Women look more for partnership and companionship in a relationship while men want to establish that they are capable of having a woman, who is "my woman", a woman who could help them wash, cook and so on. Women get into relationships so that they can help a man. Men get into relationships so that they can go and play dominoes and have the other parts of their lives taken care of by women.

The Dominica Family Planning Association started some time ago to gear a great deal of its advertising and education programmes towards men, to bring men and women together. Whether this is having any effect is difficult to say as the irresponsibility of men has its origins in school – many teachers in the primary school are women.

I myself once taught in a primary school. Before when teachers used to be males they encouraged and organized boys in cricket and so on but this has changed and there is no such organization in schools again. The female teachers concentrate on activities for girls and in schools there is now greater emphasis on academic performance, on passing the common entrance examination. More girls pass than boys, boys seem to be losing out along the way. Some subjects where boys would normally excel are not offered at CXC, subjects such as welding and auto mechanics. There seem to be more opportunities for girls to excel throughout the school system and more psychological damage to the man.

The results of this development in Dominica can be seen in the present election which has a larger number of women than ever before – 9 out of 60 candidates are women. Women are asserting themselves, taking a lead in organizations, speaking out on issues, for instance we have the National Council of Women. I don't get the sense though that men feel upset about this movement or threatened that women are taking over.

Career Opportunities and Aspirations of Women

Prostitution is not really an option for women in Dominica – to my knowledge there are no brothels, though certain women go on boats when these come in, but this is not organized. Nor are there a lot of hotels which influence the growth of this kind of trade. There has been some growth in the public services sector and together with this and teaching, there are more opportunities for women here. In addition, more women have become self- employed, baking, doing crochet, since the 1980s there has been an increase in entrepreneurial activities.

On the whole, education seems to be the number one area which women have turned to – especially higher education which is seen as a career of some sort. For that they must leave the island, many not returning, so that migration in search of education has been an aspiration of women.

The government is attempting measures to encourage people to stay on the island, as for instance working in the area of tourism. While this is going on, however, agriculture is declining as is the banana industry which is in crisis due to the European and Latin American agreements in trading in bananas, and the youth in any event do not get sufficient income from working in bananas.

Nurse Justina James, Dominica Family Planning Association

Nurse James has lived most of her life in Dominica and is committed to working in the area of family planning. She thinks that women make their own decisions about families as well as in other areas of their lives based on their own resources. This is usually dependent on the cost of living which is relatively high, and on the type of union they are in. Methods such as the 'natural' rhythm method can work with two people who live together and understand each other. Women who live in temporary unions cannot always depend on a method which does not always work. When Nurse James looks back at past generations who had larger families, she thinks it was no fault of their own. There was nothing made available to them and what they used was the old method of breastfeeding which worked for some of them. A larger family was also seen as an investment, especially if the children were boys. Previously there was a high mortality rate of children, and a higher number of miscarriages due to the hard labour which women performed (many women worked hard alongside their partners to support their families). If one looked through their life histories they had as many as three miscarriages per woman. The trend has now shifted to where women are more career con-scious, and there are larger numbers of women who use the clinic who have completed high school and college, and use both the services of the clinic and birth control methods.

Some women come to the clinic at their first pregnancy, and conversation with them shows that this pregnancy was not planned. After the first child they try not to let this occur again by getting and using contraceptives. An interesting fact was that the same women in the past who had their first children due to accidental pregnancies at age 15 or 16 and who began to use contraceptives are against the use of birth control methods by young people of today. But the women of today are very aware that they do not want to replicate their lives as a mirror of their grandmothers and mothers. For those who are career conscious, education comes first. Others try to establish themselves and their economic lives, they want land and a house and they are not dependent on men to give them these basic necessities of life. Those who are working for a reasonable income feel quite comfortable with their independence.

Q: **Is it possible to depend on men as breadwinners or responsible fathers in society?**

Women in Dominica do not see men as an "automatic" part of their lives. There are many examples around of women who are greater achievers than men in Dominica. At some point in their lives they may say they want a child just to have a child but do not wish to have a man permanently attached to their lives. Nor do they necessarily depend on the man for a subsistence or child allowance as they feel they are self-sufficient.

Q: **Of the women who come to you at the clinic, do they see childbearing as central in their lives?**

Well some of them do, in the sense that they will have one, not that they want to keep reproducing, but they make decisions which include a child and they have various things they want to do in life, but at some point they make those decisions around having a child. The age differs for different women – some decide this at age 35 for instance.

Another kind of woman who is not career conscious or self supporting, however, may find herself pregnant at an early age and the man does not want the child so the relationship does not last. They begin another relationship, and that man might say that if you love me I want you to have my child. Some try to prevent conception in cases like this but some also feel that to have the man they must give him the child he wants. The "baby father" syndrome is decreasing as women of all strata are more and more trying to prevent unwanted pregnancies. While some still go ahead and have children in an effort to keep a man, others have shifted tremendously from depending solely on one man. They try to hustle between one and two jobs at the same time to take care of the child independently of the man. "As soon as they see history repeating itself they put a stop to that."

Aspirations and Decisions of Women in Dominica

Women in Dominica enjoy being independent – they want to achieve, they are competitive with the men now, they feel they can succeed irrespective of what men might do or say. In our society, most women want to own something – they invest early. You may find young women just out of school begin to invest in land. When they are ready to settle down, that land is paid for, then they begin to invest in a house. They do not wait to be in a union to start investing and they feel good to have achieved something. They want to own their own cars, some – most – want to feel comfortable within themselves and if a man is there he is there, if he's not, he's not. Then they feel they are living life in a satisfactory way and if they take the real things they can provide for themselves to make themselves happy then they go for it.

Mrs Grell, Family Planning Educator in Dominica in her Combined Community Session/Sewing Class with a Group of Young Women

Young Woman 1: The country is hard right now and we meet to learn to sew in the hope that we could find employment in factories, or go into our own employment. The most you can do right now is learn a trade.

Migration

Nurse Grell: I think most of the people, women especially, who migrate to other countries, would like to come back, but it's just a matter of pride. If I go to the States to better myself, I make more money but I spend all of it. In Dominica, you get mango free, you get banana free, grapefruit free – you can survive. But when they realize it and if they come back people will say this and people will say that, a lot of people don't come back. My aunt went to England and she said her standard of living went down because she had to start all over again. I'm not saying that things are not hard for people here – for people who are not working and cannot buy their essential things, cannot buy their food, but for those who are working you have to know how to cut and contrive, how to make it work for you. This is what I am teaching the girls here.

Young Woman 2: I don't want to leave Dominica. I feel free here. I could go to my garden and get my provisions, in case I can't get work I could go to my mother or my sister and tell them I have a problem.

Childbearing

Young Woman 3: When you have children you have a child to keep you company at home, when your husband is out and working late in meetings and so on, you can talk to the child and play with the child. When you get old, you get your children or grandchildren to take care of you. I have no special timing to have mines, I can have them anytime.

Nurse Grell: I think in Dominica now a lot of younger people are putting off having children for education purposes. A lot of us who did not reach the heights we would have liked to reach – is because of our children. In my own career, I went to the UK when I was in my thirties, and I had left my children behind. I did not go further because I felt the need to be with my children. I advise my children now that if they like to have a family, then educate themselves first.

Long ago people think that children are an asset – that I would have a lot of children at my funeral, or when I am older I will have this child or that child. But that is when people did not travel a lot – now that people travel a lot, it is different. I know people who have seven or eight children, one in America, another one somewhere else, and they still have to get someone to take care of them. It really is not an asset the way it was before. But I agree that when they are small, children are companions, in my case my children were, but not again.

Young Woman 4: You hope if you have children then that will work, but sometimes, because of migration, they may send clothes or money, but not be there.

Young Woman 5: My mother had seven children and I only wanted one, but I got two. I wanted one child only so that I could give that child what I did not get when I was young, attention from a mother and father, the latest outfits, I want to pamper them.

Young Woman 6: Women who can't have children develop an attitude to people who have children – they feel they have so much that if they had a child they would have to share it with the child. They don't like children or other people in their house.

Young Woman 7: But some people if they don't have children also adopt. I was adopted, and so I have a child now of my own.

Nurse Grell: Traditionally we were made to believe that if we don't have children, something was wrong with you – a lot of women who did not have children, they feel left out, they feel belittled. I think this is still true. As time go on, people will change their attitudes, a lot of women already saying they don't want children.

The Dynamics of Decision Making in the Lives of Caribbean Women of Barbados, St Lucia and Dominica

To explore the dynamics of decision making related to the major events in the lives of women of Barbados, St Lucia and Dominica, and investigate the major influences affecting the process and the determinants of their aspirations, the areas examined in terms of choice were selection of partners, marriage, timing and number of children, abortion, job/career choices, education, emigration, and extracurricular activities. These variables were explored in terms of choices which women had made in their lives, against an ideal set of aspirations and goals they wanted to achieve.

The broad questions which the research set out to answer need to be restated here. These were:

1) What are the key dynamics in decision making in women's lives? Do women have autonomy in controlling their decisions or are these circum-scribed from birth by parents, class, spouse, and the social and cultural expectations of women in their particular society?

2) What are the focal points or major events in women's lives around which important decisions are taken? What do women themselves determine as the major events in their lives?

The main hypotheses which guided the gathering and analysis of data were:

1) Childbearing and childrearing still represent the major events in the lives of most Caribbean women. They may be perceived as 'natural' roles around which other choices in life may be organized. Thus decisions pertaining to work, career, family, spouse or partner, extracurricular activities and migration revolve around the centrality of childbearing.

2) The importance of childbearing as a primary definition of femininity in the Caribbean may be simultaneously undergoing change among differ-

ent groups of women in the society. Women who choose higher education and careers make more deliberate and conscious choices about deferring childbearing or setting a context for childbearing as for example with a stable partner and within a stable union. This difference may be more marked among a younger group of women than for women over a certain age threshold.

3) Women of different class or income groups have different levels of control over their lives and autonomy in decision making. Lower income women may be allowed greater societal freedom to flout social norms in order to exercise certain choices than women of higher incomes or education levels. But women with higher education and more career opportunities have the wherewithal to make autonomously some choices not available to women in low income brackets.

4) Women of all ages and socioeconomic groups are gradually shifting their concepts of femininity to incorporate notions of self-fulfillment and self-actualization of their individual goals. This may or may not include the definition of self in relation to partners; either way, this is a deliberate and conscious choice on the part of women themselves.

It is useful also to summarize the major theoretical and methodological parameters which informed the collection and analysis of data in the previous chapters. In Appendix 1 we suggest by way of recommendations other complementary studies which can be carried out for the region in order to accentuate theory, methodology and empirical findings for the region as a whole.

We attempted to move away from the dominant stereotypes adopted in previous studies on the family and of women in these societies. These stereotypes were informed by the ideology which viewed all women in the Caribbean as strong and not in need of emotional and financial support from men. Caribbean women were in general perceived as independent, strong individuals, running matrifocal households and antagonistic to their men. The main reason for deconstructing this stereotype is that it sets up a precondition for femininity in the Caribbean against which gender relations and individual women's actions are viewed. In other words, strength is perceived in terms of how a woman establishes independence from the male, how capable she is of financially and emotionally supporting her family, and dealing with the presumed irresponsibility of the Caribbean male. The resulting corollary of male irresponsibility and marginality discredits Caribbean masculinity and does a disservice to the ongoing construction of masculine identities in the region as they are developing from post slavery into contemporary times.

We also did not limit women's realities to household and family concerns, nor did we consider their household duties as non-productive in terms of the wider social output. We are therefore attempting to break down the division and walls which have been erected between private and public spheres, and which create a theoretical limitation for understanding women's lives. This theoretical limitation polarizes women into the categories of housewife versus career woman and this itself has become another unrealistic representation of woman in the emerging literature on gender. By altering the way we traditionally viewed women and the decisions they make in their lives, we are better able to recognize women's agency in their actions and choices, even when this is not readily apparent from their own interpretations of their actions. This approach validates and justifies the methods we have used to interpret the collected data, authenticating women's responses equally with other sources and valuing qualitative interpretation along with quantitative data.

An Overview of Territories Surveyed

The overview of socioeconomic data and the status of women in each of the territories pointed to some key similarities and differences between and among the three societies. On the surface, in Barbados there appear to be more opportunities for "development and change" for women. There is greater access to education especially at the tertiary level; the more sophisticated industrial climate in Barbados provides a wider scope for jobs for women, as does the expanded state sector and tourism. This situation, however, is not a stable one, dependent on foreign investment and a consistent tourist arrival. Barbados at present also has the highest unemployment rate amongst women in the three societies.

St Lucia and Dominica are more agricultural based economies although St Lucia has a growing dependency on tourism and small manufacturing industry. Manufacturing in Dominica seems to be geared to its agricultural production. Both St Lucia and Dominica have community colleges which provide first year university education, so that women from both islands still need to travel either internally in the region or externally for further university education. Women of Barbados have the choice internally in their own society. Migration from Dominica and St Lucia tends to be concentrated within the Caribbean. Migrants from these two societies also move to Barbados. Both St Lucians and Dominicans depend on Barbados for technical assistance in electricity and power technology. Barbadians migrate, to a lesser extent, to other Caribbean territories. Their horizons are more likely to be extraregional than those of St Lucians and Dominicans. As stated by one of the official respondents who were interviewed in Barbados,

Barbados appears to the islanders of St Lucia and Dominica as more developed, with people from those societies coming to Barbados to look for jobs and educational opportunities. Barbadians, by contrast, perceive the two societies of Dominica and St Lucia as fairly similar; geographically the two countries have a more rugged topography than Barbados which is essentially flat. They recognize divisions of rural and urban districts in both, and that they are both influenced by French culture.

In 1994 Barbados had the highest percentage of female-headed households (43.5 percent) compared to 40.4 percent in St Lucia and 38 percent in Dominica. Unlike Barbados and St Lucia, Dominican women who need to seek redress in law for property inheritance rights, criminal acts, violence and domestic abuse, maintenance and other disabilities have access to a wide range of legislation. The most recent changes in legislation are found in the Maintenance Act, 1981, and the Age of Majority Act, 1983. In St Lucia and Dominica, there have been no developments in the legislation regarding abortion which remains illegal. On the other hand, there are fewer developments in legislation pertaining to sexual violence. Barbados has enacted legislation prohibiting violence against women and in 1983–4 passed the Medical Termination of Pregnancy Act making abortion legal on specific grounds.

There are differences in each island in the participation of women in community based initiatives. In St Lucia there are at present 40 women's organizations and groups whose activities involve community services and family life education and a further 70 'Mothers and Fathers' groups located in rural districts also involved in community based work. Dominican women were, on the other hand, less organized at the community level but had a greater participation in top level public service positions such as magistrates and medical officers. Little evidence of a high level of community organization emerged in Barbados other than involvement in church groups and in the professions.

It is useful now to bring together the major findings from the questionnaire survey and other data collected by interviews. There is a marked decrease in the number of children which the respondents in this sample had compared to that of their parents, bearing in mind, of course, that 59.2 percent of our sample was 29 years and under and had not completed their fertility cycle. The proportion of parents in the samples who were legally married was 48 percent for Barbados, 47 percent for St Lucia and 32 percent for Dominica. The proportion of respondents in the samples who were married was 20 percent in Barbados and St Lucia and 16 percent in Dominica.

An interesting observation can be made regarding respondents' representation of their parents' unions and how they in turn describe their contemporary union status. The questionnaire had asked them to think of the kind of union which their parents had had. They described the unions of their parents in terms of married or not married, referring to the legal status of the union. In an assessment of their parents' relationships, marriage, and joint household union – as in common law relationships – in general, appeared to be approved over non-married or visiting status.

In the Caribbean, legal marriage had been traditionally viewed as attaining respectability. Marriage was seen as an achievement in later life, after the woman and man have weathered the storms of a relationship and in the meantime had had children, sometimes with partners other than the ones whom they eventually married. This study is inconclusive on the shift which has emerged in respondents' perceptions of the status of union type in the contemporary Caribbean. In most cases respondents in the survey and interviews gave unapologetic descriptions of their past and present union statuses. They were equally open on whether they were married, had common-law or visiting unions, had no relationship, were separated or divorced, and even, as in the case of two women in Dominica, had occasional partners (Table 6). This finding from the survey suggests that there has developed a healthy attitude on the part of women to the varied choice of unions they make during the cycle of their lives.

In all three societies there is a decrease in housewives from one generation to the next. Twenty-three women in Barbados, 22 in St Lucia and 39 in Dominica cited housewifery as their mothers' occupation. In contrast, five respondents in Barbados, three in St Lucia and eight in Dominica cited their occupation as that of motherhood. Thirty women in Barbados had parents who were in professional occupations as compared to vastly lower numbers in St Lucia and Dominica. Of the three countries sampled, Barbados also produced the highest number of female professionals. The data, therefore, support a clear pattern of occupational mobility between respondents and their parents. In addition there was also a wider range of occupations now available to women, compared to the choices which their mothers would have had. Many of the women in the sample were in white collar and clerical areas, occupations which required a higher level of education than their parents had had. They had also entered occupations which were not available to their mothers, such as cosmetology and NGO project officers. Many of these new jobs, however, were incompatible with childrearing thus creating an additional burden on the decision making process for women who retain the notion that childrearing is their primary responsibility. The decision becomes a more complicated one for women who do not have a steady partner to share the double burdens of childrearing and the demands of a job outside of the home.

There was a significant decrease in respondents' family size as compared to that of their parents. Of the respondents in the sample who themselves had had children, the majority had between one and three children, with only a few women in Dominica and St Lucia having up to seven children, and one woman in each of the three societies having had eight children. Among the sample, only a few of the women indicated the presence of a grandmother or aunt who assisted and was part of the extended household, and some of this assistance was temporary while they completed training for a career. It appears from the data that extended households which relied on the presence of older women to take care of children are also on the decline in family households in these territories. It may well be that many of the respondents' mothers are themselves workers out of the home, and cannot accommodate the childcare needs of their offspring. In several cases where both partners or the woman lived with either an in-law or parent, the burden of dependency brought other stresses for women. They were less free to bring up their children as they wanted and felt both imposed upon as well as imposing on other relatives' needs. This issue needs to be pursued in future studies to examine the mechanisms which women are using to organize single parent or two working partner households.

While the point has to be emphasised that only 42 of the women in the sample had completed fertility, one can draw on other factors to support the notion that women are deliberately choosing to have fewer children. First is the wide availability of different types of contraceptives in all three societies as had been indicated by the family planning officials interviewed. Contraceptives are available not only at health and family planning clinics, but also over the counter in shops and pharmacies. Greater attention is also being paid to the dissemination of information regarding the planning of families, and to creating a much greater awareness among women and men today about the advantages of contraceptive use and the benefits of smaller family size. The provision of a wider and newer range of methods of contraception has not, however, adequately dealt with the traditional attitudes to childbirth and reproduction. Family planning programmes have possibly not fully appreciated the cultural myths which still pervade this area of life. This point is supported by an observation made by Mr Willie Fevrier of Dominica: ". . . a lot of women fear using the coil as there is a rumour that the child will be born with a coil in its hand. Or for instance, with the injectable contraceptives, if women do not see the flow of menstrual blood every month, they fear that this is accumulating every month and that it is unhealthy for the body. I don't know if I really understand this concern of women." In St Lucia, Mr John La Force recalled that, "A lot of people, as late as 1977, were accusing the FPA of trying to lead young girls astray and encouraging them to spoil their lives, of killing children and of putting chemicals into their bodies. One of the reasons behind this was the importance of child bearing to women."

Nonetheless, the increased awareness and availability of contraceptives in the last two decades in the Caribbean has made for more regular use of different methods of contraceptives (see Table 9). Contraceptive use was more and more being viewed as the joint responsibility of both partners, although this varied between the three countries. In Barbados and St Lucia the decision to use contraception was either taken by the woman herself or shared jointly by both partners, while in Dominica the decision was largely taken by the woman herself. When and why they have children appear to be the growing concern of *both* men and women in the society. From the examination of planned parenthood programmes and journals published in the three societies, a new thrust has clearly been made to include the male partner as having joint responsibility and this is also having its impact. Condom use though, as a male contraceptive, is not a popular choice among men. Even with the threat of the HIV virus, men fear that the condom "will interfere with their electricity supply". By and large, the onus of using contraceptives is still on women.

This decrease in family size cannot be attributed primarily to the use or availability of contraception. It may have equally resulted from the education and career aspirations of respondents. One young respondent in Barbados indicated that she was making sure to use contraception so that she would "not get pregnant and ruin her life". Linked to the availability, must be the way in which the individual woman perceives there are larger goals which may not be reached if she has children at a very early age. There is a higher level of education among the sample for Barbados than in the other two societies and this has influenced the responses of the women in that sample. Education, by itself, however, is not the sole factor which influences the decision to have children, although it may be a reason for deferral. Some problems regarding girls' education retain a similarity for all three societies. There is a persistent notion, especially in St Lucia and Dominica, that at a certain age girls must leave school and get on with marriage, childbearing and work. Work for women is perceived under all categories from housework, childcare, domestic or farm labour, clerical, and commercial to self employment. In fact with too much frequency we found that for both these societies some of the women stated that they stopped schooling because of financial difficulties or to take care of their siblings. In these cases we found an equal lack of support for girls' education whether it was the female or male parent making the decision.

A crucial variable in the three societies surveyed which may affect women's choices to have or defer childbearing, might be the perception of education as a means to achieving a career, and the differential availability of educational opportunities in each of the islands. In Barbados the greater access to all levels of education and the longer history of educational achievement makes education a taken for granted option in this society, while education in St Lucia and Dominica is viewed as improving the quality of life. The latter is interpreted not only in relation to the type of job the woman may achieve as a result of education, but the status which is acquired with having had "education". Women with educated or professional parents who can finance their daughter's education are more likely to incorporate education and career onto their map of expectations. For women who have fewer options, accidental first and second births may be more prevalent. Education must not be viewed as an unproblematic variable in the decision to bear or not bear children. From the life stories of our respondents, greater access to education appears to have increased the dilemmas placed on womanhood and femininity, especially in societies which have not fully appreciated that infertility may have been caused by the biological condition of some women, and that the decision not to have children is also a legitimate one which each individual man or woman can make.

If childbearing is in some measure linked to level of education, then so is career choice. The responses from all three societies indicate that there is a distinct shift to higher educational attainment as well as to career choices both of which take women out of the home and into jobs sometimes incompatible with childrearing. This reduces the number or regularity with which educated and employed women choose to have children. Women in the sample who have made the choices to abort their educational goals have done so with two consequences. One is that they look after their children, then return to continue their education, beginning again as soon as domestic roles permit. On the other hand, some decide consciously that their children's education should not suffer similarly, and even if they or their mothers did not have this option, they ensure that both daughters and sons have more educational opportunities.

In some situations education and career development are linked to migration, and here women are often forced to leave children with parents, partners or other siblings, and migrate temporarily for reasons of education and career. In such cases they note that this has usually been done at the expense of the relationship with their children. They are very conscious of the reasons for the choice of leaving when they do so, seeing migration, especially from Dominica and St Lucia, as essential to furthering education and career opportunities. Migration itself appears to offer, as it always has, a means to progress and more opportunities for women for self-development. There is a mixed message which emerged from the respondents with regard to migration. While the idea of migration, whether or not children are involved, is still clearly an attractive one, offering the advantages not available in the present society, some women have internalized the disadvantages of not being in their own setting. For instance one young woman in Dominica observed "I don't want to leave Dominica, I feel free here. I could go to my garden and get my provisions, in case I can't get work I could go to my mother or my sister and tell them I have a problem". This sentiment was interestingly enough more often expressed in Dominica than in the other two islands which appear more outward looking. Nonetheless, the romantic notion of migration to the USA, and less so to the UK and Canada, still exists among many of the women in the sample, especially where lack of education and opportunities in the home country limit the scope the woman has had for self-advancement.

Where women have chosen both career and motherhood, in some cases they need to change the kind of job to allow for more flexibility of time to spend with the children. In several cases, women have said they feel that this responsibility of child care falls on them rather than on a male partner. They admit to being committed to their children despite the individual aspirations or goals they may have set for themselves. In situations with less flexibility of career choice, some women remain at home with their children until they are old enough to attend schools and take care of themselves, and then they return to the career market. In such cases they may find themselves as in the case study of Juliette of St Lucia (chapter 4), beginning at a late age to learn a skill or trade.

Caribbean Women at the Crossroads:
The Paradox of Motherhood

Sexual freedom and responsibility: From the moment the female begins an active sexual life, she is at risk of becoming a mother. Both young and older women have greater freedom to engage in sexual activity, to enter such activity on their own volition, and to openly express sexual desire. An active sexual life is linked to choice of partner and here also women are clear that by and large they exercise this choice. The majority of women in the sample in all three societies stated that their entry into first sexual activity was their own choice. This figure was 45 women in the sample for Barbados, 36 for St Lucia and 40 for Dominica. Only a few women felt pressured by partners, three in Barbados, six in St Lucia and one in Dominica. While peer pressure to begin an active sexual life is still functional (7 responses in Barbados, 12 in St Lucia and 10 in Dominica), it appears that women are consciously aware of their choices to be sexually active.

Despite relative freedom to engage in sexual activity and to choose a partner on their own, the data nonetheless show that these choices are not always informed ones. Some women become sexually active without understanding the consequences for motherhood. As indicated by one family planning official, John La Force of St Lucia, and also evident in our overall data on timing of first births, it appears that a large number of first and second births are unplanned, and only then do many women begin to plan their sexuality in relation to reproduction.

The connection between expressing their sexuality, entering a reproductive cycle and selecting a partner is an intricately linked one, even if not always recognized as such. In general, the majority of women begin an active sexual life, and have a partner whom they choose for varying reasons, one of which is that of mutual attraction. They may then have a child or children, and despite the awareness that they have made a difficult choice with respect to a partner, they usually decide to remain in this relationship. Many women do not choose to leave a union, either married or common law, until they are forced to do so.

Financial independence and the double burden: When women leave a relationship, they do so for reasons which include abuse, lack of emotional or economic support, or to develop their own careers, and usually do so only when the children have grown older. They must, however, have the wherewithal to leave a relationship before they do so, as limited financial or legal services are available to assist women in these matters, or they may have to bear the burden of child care on their own. Those women who leave a relationship with children and who choose demanding careers, or are forced by economic circumstances to enter well paid exacting jobs, now appear to be faced with a new dilemma of motherhood. The responsibility for child care and for the welfare of children still rests more heavily on the female parent than on the male. Many women now find themselves torn between the guilt of not being physically around their children more, and a resentment of men who are not made to feel similarly responsible by society, and whose career paths are less likely to be interrupted for reasons of child care. This dilemma is particularly acute in cases in which the woman's career development involves migration, where a child is left with another parent, with grandparents or other kin, or has to travel to the new society with its mother.

The idea of independence even within a union is connected with being financially secure in the event of a failure of the relationship. In other words, while historically it seems men in the Caribbean have feared that women "make children for them" to ensnare them for economic reasons, of the respondents in the sample, very few appeared to see childbearing with a partner as an automatic indication that they or their children will be supported financially. This does not imply that women do not see men as having to contribute to the upkeep of their children, but the view that women bear children as a means of economic support for themselves is a myopic one and does not consider the range of reasons why childbearing is important to women, both in terms of expressing their feminine identity, and in their perception of the improved quality of the relationship between partners who have children together.

It appears, however, that women consciously go into relationships with the idea that they do not want to be financially dependent, and in the responses we find the majority of women voicing this as a precondition for a relationship.

Representing femininity: Childbearing remains central to women. It is viewed as an affirmation of life and for the continuity of human society, even if not articulated in these ways by the average man or woman. This need to reproduce has been rooted in culture and carried across generations through myth and symbols. For example John La Force draws attention to these:

There was some myth, may be out of religion, that if a woman does not have a child, she is cursed in some way, so every woman must try to have her womb blessed by having a child. A woman is not complete without a child. I know many women who do not have a child, they deferred childbearing because of a career. And other women would chastise them and say you're cursed, you can't even have a child. There were even names for women who could not have children.

The motivation to reproduce seems to derive from biology, to be located in cultural customs, to be linked to the definition of femininity among women and men, and to the social sanctions imposed on the individual who does not bear a child. There is also the idea that childbearing is important for the psychological and emotional growth of a woman. As Glenda from Barbados puts this: "You don't realize how mortal you are till you have children. You are always praying that nothing happens to you. You get a mortality check the day you give birth." Childbearing and centering one's priorities around the needs of a child appear to provide women with both the strength and convictions to be good mothers, to work and value relationships with their children and other women, and thus concretize the ideas on which the "nature" of femininity is built. Within this construct, childbearing is equally central for another reason – that of economics. Some women view children as economic support in their declining years, although this perception is simultaneously undergoing change as women see families breaking up and moving far away. Another crucial reason for childbearing for women is the idea of children as emotional support with or without a resident partner. Thus childbearing remains very central in a culture where the dominant ideology from one generation to the next is that children are more important to the life of the individual, than are emotional relationships based on sexual unions.

What is definitely undergoing change is that each of these features is waxing or waning in importance with "development". First, the economic difficulties of bringing up many children or even one child if finance and time do not permit more; secondly, the myths are losing ground in situations where women demonstrate satisfaction with careers and comfort with their independence. It is clearly becoming more acceptable for women to choose to defer childbearing until they can accommodate another dependent. Thus we feel that femininity is no longer completely linked to evidence of fertility. "Womanhood" is also being valued in terms of competence in non-traditional spheres.

Alongside traditional ideas, what women are now presented with are alternatives. These include the decisions to have children early, to defer childbearing, and to choose to not have children at all. In all of these possibilities, it appears that the shift has been to a more individuated decision, or a decision worked out in relation to a male partner where emotional support is forthcoming. While social norms continue to prescribe the boundaries allowed to women with respect to the definition of their femininity, the legacy of matrifocality is that it centres the decision making and responsibility for the outcomes on the woman herself. The presence or absence of the male partner in the rearing of the child and in the continued financial, social and emotional world of the woman is not a taken for granted assumption, if it ever was.

For those women who have consciously chosen careers instead of early motherhood, the question of whether or not to have children, when to time them, with whom to have them, become new dilemmas. For many women the question is not that they do not want a child, but how they cope with a child and the demands of a career or other goals they have set themselves. Children may therefore be viewed as an obstacle to such goals. For those who make informed choices about childbearing, the problem is not primarily that of giving birth but of the arrangements for childrearing. The paradox of motherhood faced by the women in the sample is that they perceive childbearing as still important to their feminine identity and to the biological life cycle, but that they also recognize that children may be a deterrent in their achievement of certain goals and aspirations which they may have set for themselves.

Ironies of feminism: With the growing concern and need for career and self-development among women, additional emotional burdens are being placed on those women who wish to choose housewifery and motherhood as careers. They begin to assimilate notions of inferiority in relation to their female peers who have chosen other careers, and become defensive of their choices. This has not been one of the healthy outcomes of feminism in the latter half of the twentieth century and perhaps needs to be deliberately addressed. As we attempt to break down the hierarchy between public and private spheres are we persistently devaluing those activities, such as housework and childcare, which generally take place in the "private" individual setting? In other words, childbearing, childrearing and domestic tasks need to be equally validated along with careers outside of the home. In this respect one of the shifts which seems to be occurring is the extent to which women are seeking self-employment and creating jobs for themselves, not only to cope with increasing unemployment, but to deal with the dilemmas of choice between mothering and career. Only thus are they able to deal with the guilt placed on them by society of not being good mothers, having organized their time to handle domestic arrangements and crises.

Redefining femininity and accommodating differences: A significant point which emerges in this study, however, is the difference among women themselves with regard to issues of partnership, type of union and childbearing. Several women (the case of Virginia in St Lucia is representative of this), have made distinctions between choices *vis- à-vis* sexual activity, reproduction, career and union status. By this we mean that they are aware of the consequences of each of their choices and tend to be so from an early age, so that the occurrence of a first pregnancy and first birth does not form the crux around which life choices are then centred. In other words, their choices may follow other paths: of education, career, intermittent partners, migration, return and career, visiting or occasional partners, and the desire to have a child around the age of 30, whether with or without a residential partner. The latter scenario appears to be the choice of only a smaller number of women in the sample, since there are also women who still feel that childbearing and a joint union are central to a woman's life and to the definition of femininity. This was evident for instance in the group of young women in Dominica who were interviewed collectively, who held traditional views on the conditions for childbearing and childrearing.

What emerges when we pool the collective data on sexuality, childbearing, education, career aspirations and migration, is a common notion shared by all the women that these areas of their lives are ones in which major decisions are made. There is no sequential order by which all women can sometimes make these decisions, and this definitely differs depending on the country and socioeconomic position of the woman concerned. For instance a woman born into a family in which either the father or mother, or both, have professions is very likely to defer childbearing, continue education up until tertiary level, possibly migrate during this period of education, find a job, and then begin her childbearing. These differences were illustrated by the case studies of Glenda and Mary. The woman who is born into a family of farmworkers, domestics or tradespersons may have to stop schooling in the middle of her secondary education, find a job to help support her family and may also begin childbearing herself. Her choices at an early age are not so much calculated as they are, by and large, made for her by the economic and social circumstances around her. The exceptions, however, are always to be found where women come from non-professional families, but their goals are defined first in terms of career and education rather than primarily around childbearing.

The major obstacles women have pointed to which have delimited or informed their choices have been first, the presence of children in their lives, second, limited education, followed by lack of employment and opportunities in areas of interest, family responsibilities, money and time. These were all interconnected obstacles in the lives of the women and could not be artificially separated. While women are faced with constraints, they nonetheless have aspirations which continuously inform the decisions and choices they make. Decisions are arrived at by negotiating between the situation of their birth and ongoing experience, with a culturally accepted or individual ideal of feminine identity. Experience works differently for different women. For example a perception of her mother's limited life chances and unhappy union might influence a young woman towards ideas of independence which another woman arrives at only after she herself has experienced certain difficulties in life. In each society we examined there is also a concurrent process at work. Some women consciously make choices at a very early age to have education and a career, and they have the resources to develop in these areas, before they include childbearing in the cycle of their lives. Other women may or may not make these conscious choices, nor have the where-withal to plan career as well as childbearing. Both sets of women work with the circumstances which are present in their lives, centring each decision around how it affects the presence or absence of children. Such decisions may include partners for a temporary period of their lives, but may not always hinge around a resident partner. Women often choose to leave a relationship in which their aspirations are not being met.

Linking with men . . . connecting masculinity: This idea of female independence is matched by a finding which emerged on male attitudes to children and women. If femininity is linked to evidence of childbearing, then so is masculinity in the Caribbean. Manhood is perhaps defined in relation to having a child or children with one or several women. What emerges in the voices of the women and the experience of family planning officials is that while many men feel responsible for their children, they are not similarly responsible to the union or relationship within which the child is born. Part of this irresponsibility appears to be the result of the history of gender relations in the region and the ideology of matrifocality. Women are viewed as 'naturally' antagonistic to men, and are perceived by men as adults, capable of taking care of their own emotional and financial state. In other words men are more likely to see themselves as fathers rather than as husbands or partners. Fathering for some men involves biologically fathering a child; for others, it includes the responsibility for care and upbringing of the child. While it is certain that not all men hold antagonistic views towards women, and in fact many show signs of wishing to meet women's aspirations to joint partnerships, distrust still seems to be a dominant feature of gender relations in the Caribbean.

The changes which are gradually emerging in the definition of femininity are nonetheless provoking a redefinition of masculinity. Masculinity and femininity exist not only as polar opposites, premised on antagonism. Masculinity and femininity also exist as relational categories of gender identity. Historically, male sexual freedom has not been generally associated with responsibility either to partners or to offspring, whereas it has been incumbent on the female to accept this responsibility. One of the more promising outcomes of the shifts in femininity has been the challenges to masculinity. Gender relations are being re-negotiated as more and more women increasingly achieve financial independence and recognition as indispensable contributors to the household. This raises the question then: what are the demands and responsibilities of the male in terms of partnerships, childbearing and childrearing?

The Dynamics of Decision Making

The study has set out to identify, collate and analyse the data in the areas which women deem are either important to their lives, or where they make decisions. The final consideration here is to suggest ideas on the dynamics of choice, or how women make the decisions that they do. This must be set against the last hypothesis proposed in the theoretical framework, that these choices are part of the process of constructing femininity among Caribbean womanhood which is not completely linked to the traditional ideas of motherhood or wifehood. In other words, while woman has been seen in relation to children or partner, the study reveals other dynamics which work within the life experience of any individual woman. The first point to be highlighted is that women work within a series of constraints, an idea of femininity, delinked partially from childbearing, but one which is also undergoing change. While women of different socioeconomic status are clearly presented with dissimilar sets of resources or limitations, the biological notions of reproduction are nonetheless foremost in their minds, whether it is to defer childbearing, to have children on their own without a partner, or to not have children at all. What women appear to do persistently is to make the best of the circumstances in which they are located, and to do so in pragmatic ways, as for instance finding support for children while they temporarily migrate.

The second major point might be that women now perceive their lives consciously in terms of both childbearing and career. That is, they may in fact combine these roles but do so actively and as a deliberate choice. Thus their actions do not seem to be ad hoc arrangements which are imposed by the decisions or needs of others around them. Even without articulating this in their own lives, they have prioritized certain needs and goals and set about achieving this in a somewhat linear fashion. For example, if childbearing has limited education and career, women ensure that they first meet their responsibilities, then plan for another stage in their lives. This goal of continuously planning for the future seems to be the basis on which they operate, and appears to also underlie the difference of femininity from masculinity as it is being constructed in the Caribbean today. For instance almost all of the male officials interviewed noted that women succeed at the things they set out to do, that they are becoming more educated than the men, that they are more responsible as parents and that men are in a state of growing crisis. Since this crisis is an external one, not the making of the individual man and woman and rooted primarily in shifting socioeconomic conditions, it appears that women are making choices constantly to meet the changing demands of society. In doing so they challenge the norms which have traditionally defined their roles. This consciousness appears to be existent in women of all ages, with women of an older age group perhaps arriving at some knowledge of themselves differently, and later in life, after initial experiences.

Given the centrality of childbearing which this study has proven, within the context of other possibilities for self-actualization in the region which have included education, migration, and careers, it appears that planned parenthood programmes cannot be unproblematically envisaged as a mechanical application of education and contraceptive choices. The bombardment of family planning contraceptive choice has not fully appreciated the complexity with which decisions are made. While family planning programmes have tried to keep up to date with the changing climate of sexuality and sexual choice, and are informed by the concerns of development of human and scarce resources in society, it appears that choices which both women and men make about their lives revolve around other crucial ideologies and factors in society. The economic realities of unemployment, low wages, the higher cost of bringing up children, the opportunities they have missed which they would like to make available to their own children, the inconsistency of sexual unions, and the incompatibility of combining a double burden of work outside and inside the home, have clearly made an impact on the minds of women who have historically borne the major part of the burden of childrearing in the region. Allied with this has been a new notion of independence defined by women themselves, an independence which must not be dismissed as selfish, or selfserving, but which is located in their desire to not be dependent. Dependency denotes lack of power. Power is viewed as the capacity to assist their families and achieve individual goals beyond the confines of their families. Power is also now being viewed as the capacity to enter into decision making in the political and wider socioeconomic spheres where policies are made which affect their lives as well as their children's.

Some women are cognitively aware of the connections between their reproductive lives and the life chances of their children, and others are not. As it has been demonstrated, the majority of women still begin to formulate plans after the birth of their first and second children. It appears to us that for these women, childbearing is the more crucial dimension to defining a full and rounded life, and decisions pertaining to their other aspirations in life are taken after, in relation to the needs and existence of their children.

Among those who defer childbearing, the dilemmas emerge later, in the form of demanding careers, absence of partners who are suitably matched and social expectations of their class which still disallow single parenthood (which itself is changing rapidly in the Caribbean). Then their decisions about whether to have or not have children become sometimes academic, influenced by the strength of their aspirations for their future, and by having experienced more of life itself. In this respect there may be an age threshold at which change is occurring and the data suggest that women of age 35 and under, in other words the younger generation in the region, are accelerating these shifts, regardless of territory. The shift may be contingent on factors which are more global, as opposed to cultural specificities in the societies surveyed.

The dynamics of choice seem to work hand in hand with aspirations for a full life and goals which people predetermine for themselves. Opportunities for education and self-fulfillment influence the kind of aspirations people mentally formulate, and these are both individual freedoms as in independence, as well as material goals – for jobs, financial security and comfortable lives. The pragmatism evident in the past construction of femininity in the region has prepared women to match aspirations with the existing conditions. Thus they continue to work within the immediate constraints, with each new generation pushing the boundaries of gender identity a bit further.

This process does not appear to have worked similarly with masculinity which is framed with more boundaries. Man has remained more confined to patriarchal notions of masculine privileges. Thus and only thus can we explain the way in which women in the contemporary setting of the three societies have made virtue out of necessity, persistently confronting many adversities to map out meaningful goals, and make informed decisions about their lives. They continue to face life in these societies with joy and resilience, with warmth and affection for other women, and for their supportive or itinerant menfolk. This has been the dominant feature of womanhood we encountered in our interviews, and in our brief sojourn with the many respondents with whom we came into contact in the islands of Barbados, St Lucia and Dominica.

Bibliography

Anderson, Pat. 1986. "Conclusion: WICP". *Social and Economic Studies* 35 no. 2: 291-324.

Barbados Family Planning Association. *The Family Magazine*. December 1993.

Barrow, Christine. 1986. "Finding the support: strategies for survival". *Social and Economic Studies* 35 no. 2: 131–76.

Byron, Margaret. 1994. *Post-War Caribbean Migration to Britain: the Unfinished Cycle*. Aldershot, Brookfield: Avebury Ashgate Publishing Co.

Cable & Wireless. *The Caribbean Handbook 1995/96*. Researched and edited by Lindsay Maxwell FT Caribbean (BVI) Ltd.

Clarke, Edith. 1979. *My Mother who Fathered Me: a Study of the Family in Three Selected Communities in Jamaica*. London: Allen & Unwin.

Country Environmental Profile: St Lucia. 1991. The Caribbean Conservation Association on behalf of the Government of St Lucia.

Dominica National Council on Women. 1994. "Report on the Status of Women in the Commonwealth of Dominica". Prepared by the Dominica National Council on Women (DNCW).

ECLAC. 1989. "Comparative Status of Women in Selected Caribbean Countries as Indicated by Selected Social, Economic, Demographic and Legal Parameters".

ECLAC. 1994. "Achieving Social Justice, Equality and Development: a Review of the Status of Women of the Caribbean Subregion in Preparation for the 4th World Conference on Women, 1995".

ILO & CARICOM. 1995. *Women, Labour and the Law: a Caribbean Perspective*.

Leo-Rhynie, Elsa. 1994. "The Family in Jamaica". Prepared for the Commonwealth Secretariat for International Year of the Family 1994.

Lynch, Roslyn. 1995. *Gender Segregation in the Barbadian Labour Market 1946 and 1980*. Kingston, Jamaica: Consortium Graduate School with Canoe Press, UWI.

Massiah, Joycelin. 1986. "Women in the Caribbean Project: an Overview". *Social and Economic Studies* 35 no. 2: 1–29.

Mohammed, Patricia. 1988. "The Caribbean Family Revisited". In *Gender in Caribbean Development*, edited by P. Mohammed and C. Shepherd. Trinidad: University of the West Indies/Women & Development Studies Group.

Mondesire, Alicia, and Leith Dunn. 1995. *Towards Equity in Development: a Report on the Status of Women in Sixteen Commonwealth Caribbean Countries*. Georgetown, Guyana: Caribbean Community Secretariat.

Momsen, Janet. 1993. *Women and Change in the Caribbean: a Pan-Caribbean Perspective.* Kingston: Ian Randle Publishers; Indianapolis: Indiana University Press; London: James Currey.

Ministry of Legal Affairs and Women's Affairs. 1994. "National Report on the Status of Women: Saint Lucia: Executive Summary". Prepared for the United Nations Conference on Women, Beijing, China by the Ministry of Legal Affairs & Women's Affairs.

Powell, Dorian. 1986. "Caribbean women and their response to familial experiences". *Social and Economic Studies* 35 no. 2: 83–130.

Ministry of Legal Affairs and Women's Affairs. 1994. "Rare Centre's Family Planning Initiative". In collaboration with St Lucia Planned Parenthood Federation, National Population Unit, Ministry of Health & Ministry of Women's Affairs. August (draft).

Rawlins, Joan. 1987. "Sexuality, contraception and the family". Paper presented at the first Interdisciplinary Seminar on Gender, Culture and Caribbean Development, UWI.

Senior, Olive. 1991. *Working Miracles: Women's Lives in the English-Speaking Caribbean.* Bridgetown, Barbados, Indianapolis: ISER with Indiana University Press.

Smith, R. T. 1956. *The Negro Family in British Guiana: Family Structure and Social Status in the Villages*. London: Routledge.

United Nations Conference on Women, Beijing, China. By the Ministry of Legal Affairs and Women's Affairs. 17 August 1994.

UNDP. 1993. *Country Human Development Indicators*.

The Courier no. 140, 1993.

Contemporary Newspapers of the Three Societies
Barbados

Daily Nation Tuesday, 14 February 1995

Daily Nation Monday, 27 February 1995

Daily Nation Wednesday, 1 March 1995

The Barbados Advocate Wednesday, 1 March 1995

The Barbados Advocate Friday, 3 March 1995

St Lucia

The Voice Tuesday, 14 February 1995

The Voice Thursday, 16 February 1995

The Weekend Voice Saturday, 18 February 1995

The Weekend Voice Saturday, 25 February 1995

Dominica

Tropical Star Vol 2 no. 18 Wednesday, 15 February 1995

Tropical Star Vol. 2 no. 19 Wednesday, 22 February 1995

The New Chronicle Vol. LXXXVII no. 7 Friday, 17 February 1995

Appendix

I

Recommendations

The recommendations cited here relate to gaps in the research data which it is hoped further studies will address.

1. This study presents a continuity from the WICP methodology (1979–1982). Unlike the WICP which used larger samples and was more comprehensive, the initial findings of this study suggest that we need to replicate studies such as this for other countries, including larger Caribbean territories in order to assess the changing climate for the definition of femininity in the Caribbean and thus for the factors which facilitate or limit women's choices in the larger setting. Is it that smaller islands limit or constrain women more than larger ones or would the findings be similar for all societies in the Caribbean?

2. The study has only touched the surface of an issue which family planning programmes have been dealing with for three to four decades in the Caribbean. How and why do women choose or not choose to have children, how they plan their families and what approaches can be used for targetting women in education and information programmes of the Planned Parenthood Federation? The first point is that such programmes need to be very conversant with the socioeconomic and ideological changes which are taking place in the society and how they affect women in their daily lives. Thus, for instance, a focus on reducing family size rests on the assumption that women have desired large families. The idea here is that programmes need to work with the notion that a woman's choice regarding reproduction is one among many which she may be prioritizing equally in her life.

3. The researchers were struck by the way in which abortion in these societies was treated as either sanctioned or illegal, or a subject to be hidden behind closed doors. While the study did not set out to pursue the understanding of this very complex issue in these societies, we were appalled at some of the popular notions which surrounded the issue as for example that "some

129

women use abortion as contraception". This area remains a troublesome one in the sphere of reproduction. It also remains a contentious and controversial one in the area of health and reproduction policies in these islands and elsewhere. It is hoped that this is also one of the issues pertaining to reproduction and to women's lives which will be undertaken for further study by the IPPF and organizations of this kind.

4. Finally, while the study focused on women and came closer to understanding the ongoing redefinition of femininity in Caribbean society, a similar project is clearly needed to understand the role of men in the decision making of women and vice versa. Since the focus of the study was on women, the respondents were largely women and their testimonies were drawn on here, it was not possible to see how women's choices and decisions are affected, fully or in part, by their relationships with men. Reproduction, in general, requires the coupling of both sexes, and the study has revealed that despite change and development, childbearing remains central to the goals of most women. Whether male attitudes to reproduction and childcare are also shifting has not been pursued fully in this study, although some insights from the data gathered here have indicated that there are tendencies towards change. We feel that future studies like this should also be attempted to bring the voices of women in dialogue with men. In other words we should be examining simultaneously how decisions are made by one sex in relation to the other: how men and women are continuously negotiating the boundaries of masculinity and femininity within each culture.

Appendix

II

Questionnaire

This comprises the instrument which was used in the questionnaire interview with the 375 respondents. For purposes of presentation as an appendix to the study, the spaces actually provided for the responses have been reduced.

CONFIDENTIAL

INTERNATIONAL PLANNED PARENTHOOD FEDERATION STUDY

Executing Agent: Dr Patricia Mohammed, Centre for Gender and Development Studies, University of the West Indies, Mona, Jamaica.

Title of study   The Dynamics of Decision making in the lives of Caribbean Women, with special reference to Barbados, St Lucia and Dominica

[Would you agree to give me information on your name, address etc. and also to a longer interview at a future date which will be taped as well?]

A. PRELIMINARIES

Name of person interviewed _____

Address_____

Contact Information (Tel, fax, etc) _____

Age_____   Year of Birth_____

Place of birth: (If different from Address) _____

Can you tell me something about both your parents? (PROMPT in this order if possible: age, kind of union/marriage, economic status/occupation, how many children?)

B. EDUCATION

(2)   What schools have you attended? (PROMPT: type of schools and level of education) _____

(3)   About how many years of schooling have you had? _____

(4)   What level of schooling have you achieved? _____

[Only if respondent went up to primary level ask questions 5, 6 and 7; if not, move on immediately from (4) to (8) and (9)]

(5)   Why did you stop going to school? _____

(6)   Would you have liked to continue your education?_____

(7)   If yes, why?_____

(8)   What subjects did you pursue at different levels of education: _____

(9)   Are these the subjects you were personally interested in? If so, why? (PROMPT if necessary; any influence of mother or father or anyone else?) _____

C. CAREER HISTORY

(10) What was your first job? _____

(11) What were your reasons for selecting this job? _____

(12) Did you have other ambitions or other jobs to choose from at the time you started your first job?_____ If so what were these? _____

(13) Did you move on to other jobs after your first one, and when was this? (chronological order) _____

(14) What were your reasons for changing jobs?_____

(15) Have there been periods when you were not working outside of the home?_____

(16) If so, why and what were you doing? _____

(17) When you were not working outside of the home what were your means of support? _____

(18) Did you feel less in charge of your life as a result of not bringing in an income? _____

(19) Do you think work is important to a woman and, if so why? _____

D. MIGRATION HISTORY

(20) Have you ever had to move from one place to another or one country to another at any time? _____

If so, when and where did you move to?_____

(21) Did you think that the opportunities you would have as a woman would be greater in another Caribbean island? If so which island or islands and why? _____

(22) Did you think your opportunities for advancement would be better out of the Caribbean, if so, where and why? _____

(23) If you have moved from one place to another, why did you do so? (PROMPT: Was it because of your relationship, children, job, health, etc.?) _____

(24) Who made the decisions about moving? _____

(25) Did this move have any effect on your career, family, friendships and so on? (PROMPT: especially arrangements re children) _____

E. PERSONAL HISTORY

Please assure respondent about confidentiality again and freedom to not answer any questions if they so choose.

(26) At what age did you start menstruating? _____

(27) Who told you about the "facts of life"? (PROMPT: parents, friends, teachers, books) _____

(28) At what age were you sexually active? _____

(29) Why? (PROMPT: did you feel social pressures for conforming? etc.)

(30) Are you married or living with someone at present? _____If so, what kind of relationship do you have at the moment? _____

(31) If you have a partner at present, (or of the partner/s you have had) what made you choose this (these) person(s) as a partner? _____

(32) Did you find after you were in the relationship for a while, that you had made the right choice of partner? If yes or no, what are your reasons for thinking this was right or wrong for you? _____

(33) What are the things about your partner or partners which have satisfied your needs in a relationship? _____

(34) At what age did you either get married or begin your full-time relationship? _____

Do you think that this first choice was because of your age and experience of gender relations at the time? _____

(35) Why did you get married or live with someone? Was it your own choice to do so or were there other reasons which made it necessary to do so? _____

(36) If you did not marry, or live with someone, why was this so? _____

(37) Do you have other significant relationships (eg other partners, good friends, outside of your stable relationship?_____ If so why (PROMPT: economic reasons, emotional support) _____

(38) Do you have any children? _____ If yes, when did you have your first child and how many children do you have? _____ What are their ages?_____

(39) Are they all with the same partner? _____(If they are not, PROMPT: where is/are the father/s?) _____

(40) Were the children born before, during or after your stable union? _____

(41) Who made the decision to have a child or children? Was it you or your partner(s) or did you decide together? _____

(42) Did you or your partner(s) decide whether contraception was to be used, and if so what method should be used _____

(43) Did you want to have children and if so why? _____

(44) Did your partner want children and if yes or no, why? _____

(45) If you did have children were they planned for or were they accidentally conceived and what was the response of your partner? _____

(46) Did having children affect your relationship with your partner? Was it better or worse and if so how?_____

(47) Would you have any problems telling me if you have you had any abortions? _____

If so, would you be willing to say where this was done? _____

(48) Whose decision was it that you should have an abortion (yours, partner's, mother's, father's, etc.) _____

(49) Does your partner assist you with the care and needs of your children or household? _____ If yes how do you share this task? _____

(50) Do the children live with you alone? _____

If yes why is this so? _____

(51) If the children live with you, how do you cope with their needs? (PROMPT: economic, emotional, social, etc.) _____

(52) Does your partner (absent or live in) contribute in any way to the upbringing of the children? If so how, and if not, why not?_____

(53) Do you need to depend on others to help with your own economic needs and your children's upbringing, for example, the government, relatives and so on. If so why, and in what ways?_____

F. EXTRACURRICULAR ACTIVITIES

(54) Do you have any special interests or hobbies outside of career and family? If so, what are these? (PROMPT: includes church groups, other organizations/activities) _____

(55) Have you been actively pursuing these interests? If not, why not?_____

(56) What in your opinion are the most important decisions you have made in your life? _____

(57) How would you rate these decisions in terms of importance to you? (PROMPT – only if necessary – reminders of what interviewee said in terms of children, education, etc.) _____

(58) What do you think have been the major obstacles in your life limiting the things you wanted to do so far? _____

(59) If you were not limited by anything, money, place of residence, education and so on, what kind of life would you like to have as a woman?_____

Any other comments from interviewee _____

[Interviewer's assessment of race and social class of interviewee] _____

END OF QUESTIONNAIRE

Appendix III

List of interviewers and official sources in the three islands

Barbados

Mr Charles Pilgrim	Executive Director, Barbados Family Planning Association & IPPF Representative
Ms Roseanne Richards	(Questionnaire Interviewer) Guidance Counsellor, Alleyne High School, Barbados
Ms Joan Cuffie	(Questionnaire Interviewer) Coordinator, Women & Development Studies & Lecturer in the Faculty of Education

St Lucia

Mr John La Force	Executive Director, St Lucia Family Planning Association & IPPF Representative
Dr Seurage	President, St Lucia Planned Parenthood Federation
Ms Cecilia Prospere	(Questionnaire Interviewer) Community Development Officer, Ministry of Youth and Community Development
Mr Jim Xavier	(Questionnaire Interviewer) Community Development Officer, Ministry of Youth and Community Development
Mr M. Pascal	(Questionnaire Interviewer) Community Development Officer, Ministry of Youth and Community Development

Dominica

Mr Willie Fevrier	Executive Director, Dominica Family Planning Association & IPPF Representative

Ms Martha Joseph   (Questionnaire Interviewer) Training and worker in community development

Nurse Justina James   Dominica Family Planning Association

Mrs Grell Family   Planning Educator (this interview was conducted in her community session with a group of young women which was combined with a sewing class)

Location of Barbados, St Lucia and Dominica in the Caribbean region and relevant geographical details of the three societies

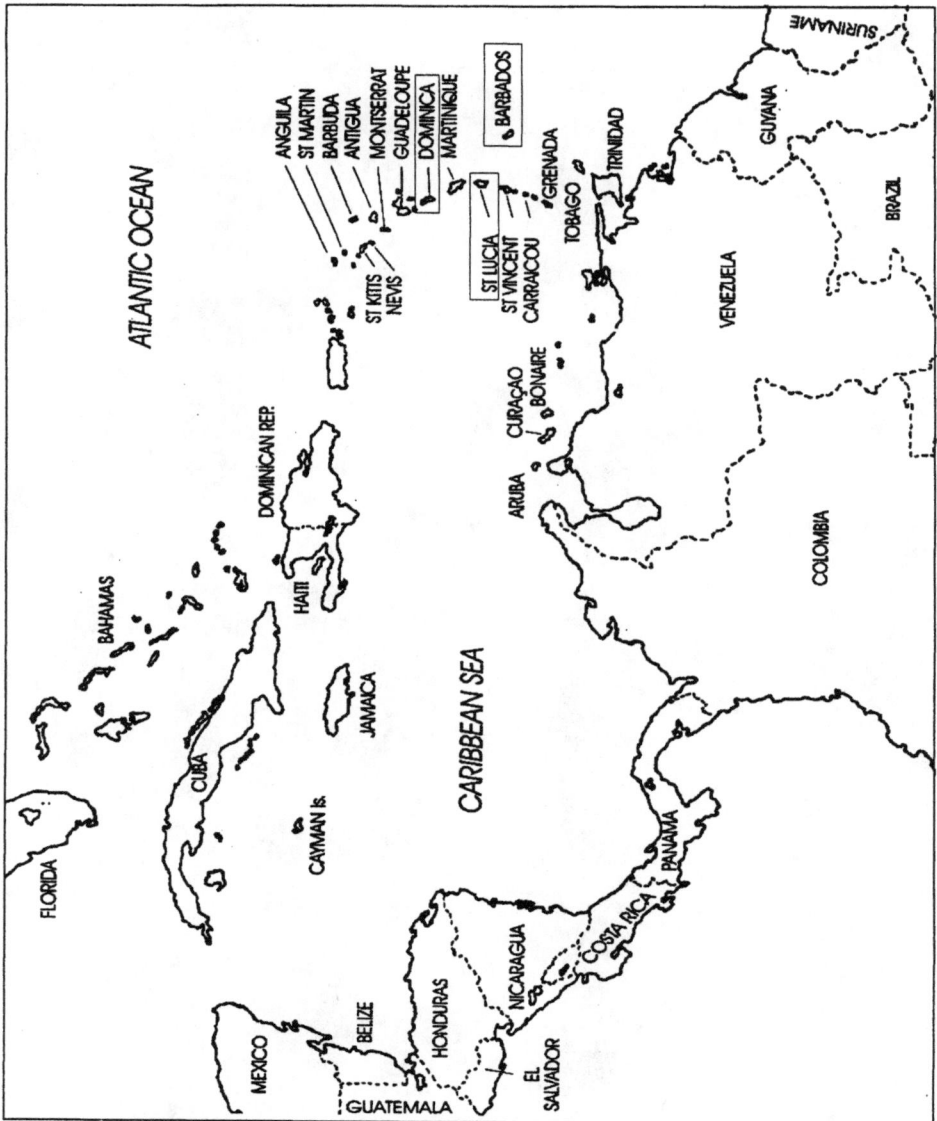

The Caribbean

Index

Abortions, 64-65, 73, 96-97, 100, 129; attitudes, 64, 73, 97; knowledge, 64-65; legislation, 35, 96-97; male attitudes to, 100

Anderson, Patricia, 5

Barbados: demographic location, 34; economic viability, 34; education, 35, 48, 70, 71 (*see also* Women); employment, 35 (*see also* Career); legislation, 35, 96-97, 113; migration, 54-55; occuptions, 46, 47, 48, 50 (*see also* Career); personal life histories, 82-86; socioecoomic profile, 34-35

Barrow, Christine, 4, 5

Byron, Margaret, 41

Career and Education, ix, 35, 40, 44, 48, 49, 50, 70, 71, 75, 79-80, 83-84, 89

Centrality, 4, 11, 110, 124

Childbearing, 3-6, 11, 61-65, 69, 70, 71-72, 104,115-126. *See also* Men and Women

Child rearing, 11, 114, 124

Clarke, Edith, 1, 2, 5

Contraceptives: method, 63; use, 34, 37, 62-64, 96, 99-101, 103

Decision making, 3-7, 5, 11-12, 63-64, 68, 72, 106, 123. *See also* Men and Women

Dynamics, viii, ix, 6, 8, 9, 11, 12, 13, 63, 110, 123,125

Dilemma, 2, 116, 125

Dominica: demographic location and make-up, 38; economic viability, 39-40; education, 40, 48, 49, 50, 70; legislation, 40; migration, 56-57, 104; occupations, 47, 48, 52-53 (*see also* Career); personal histories, 91-95, 108-109; socioeconomic profile, 38

Education, 35, 40, 48, 49, 50, 70, 71. *See also* country headings, and Women

Employment, 34, 36, 38, 40, 41, 75. *See also* country occupations

Family: history, 45-47, 53, 60 ; organization in the Caribbean, 1, 2; size, 7, 39, 47, 61, 103-104, 106, 114 decrease in, 103-104, 115, 116, 129

Family planning, 91, 96-97, 99-109, 124, 129

Family Planning Clinics, 12, 13, 96, 103, 115

Female headship, 7, 9, 39, 113

Feminism, 10, 119, 121

Femininity: construction of, ix, 4, 8, 10, 11, 12, 70-71, 116

Fertility: rates, ix, 34, 39, 61,115; completed, ix, 10, 40, 44, 61, 115

Gender identity, 8, 70

Gender (sexual) equality, 8

Gender research methodology, 7-14, 110-112; limitations and strengths, 14

International Planned Parenthood
Federation viii, 130
Ideology: gender, 3, 7; colonial 2, 8

Leo-Rhynie, Elsa, 7

Makiesky-Barrow, Susan, 5
Marital status: common law, 1, 39,
45–46, 47, 60–61, 114; legal union, 1, 39,
45–46, 47, 60–61, 113
Marriage, 45-46, 60, 83. *See also* family
history and oral history
Massiah, Joycelin, 3, 6
Matrifocal, 1, 2, 7, 8, 9, 111; matrifocal-
ity, 1, 8, 9 ; stereotype, 2, 8, 9
Marginality (male), ix, 1, 7, 8, 111
Masculinity, 8, 10, 103-104, 111, 130
Men: decision making, 5, 63, 123 (*see
also* childbearing); migration, 41;
occupational choices, 47
Migration, 41-43, 54-57, 101, 104, 117
(*see also* country headings); internal, 41,
54–55; external, 41-42, 54-55, 104
Momsen, Janet, 6, 7
Mohammed, Patricia, 2
Motherhood, ix, 1, 4, 18, 76, 81
Myth, 5, 99, 103, 115, 119

Obeah (*garde*), 99
Obstacles, 73-76, 122, 94
Occupational choices, 46-47, 50 (*see also*
Men and Women); housewife, 46, 114;
mobility, 46-47, 114; teaching, 46
Oral histories, 82-95

Paradox, 7, 9, 118
Parents, viii, 39, 45-47, 113
Patriarchy, 4, 6 ,7, 9, 11
Photographs, 15-31
Powell, Dorian, 4
Pregnancy, 37, 48, 49, 53, 86, 100,106,
Public/Private dichotomy, 5, 10

Rawlins, Joan, 7
Relationships, 45, 71, 86. *See also* Oral
histories
Religion, 35, 71; Christianity, 71; Roman
Catholic, 35, 103, 118; Anglican, 35

Senior, Olive, 3, 4, 76
Sexual activity, 57-65, 72
Sexual division of labour, 51
Sexuality, ix, 67, 72, 102; first sexual
experience, 57- 60
Smith R.T., 1
St Lucia: demographic make-up, 36;
economic viability, 36; education, 48-49,
70 (*see also* Women); migration, 56;
occupations, 46-47, 48-49, 52 (*see also*
Career); personal life histories, 87–91;
socioeconomic profile, 36; improvements for
women, 37
Sutton, Constance, 5

Union: marriage, 1– 2, 4; legal, 1;
concubinage, 2

Women: aspirations and goals, 76-81,
82-95, 107, 121; education, 48-50,
70-71, 75, 79-80. *See also* headings
under each country; extra-curricular
activities, 65-67; decision making, 3-7,
9, 11–12, 72, 106 (*see also* Childbearing
and Personal life histories); independence,
7; migration,41-43, 54–57; obstacles
affecting women, 73–76, 122; occupational
choices, 46–47, 50; personal life histories,
82–95 (*see also* family history); political
activity, 77–79; self improvement, 71
Women in the Caribbean Project, (WICP)
2-5, 45, 129

Young women, 10, 44, 59, 101, 102, 107